TO: Joyce

to my/our m

Bob

MW00471288

What a Way to Make
A Living

ASA Publishing Corporation
An Accredited Publishing House with the BBB
www.asapublishingcorporation.com

The Landmark Building
23 E. Front St., Suite 103, Monroe, Michigan 48161

Copyrights©2018 Franklin R. Jackes, All Rights Reserved
Book Title: What a Way to Make a Living
Date Published: 04.24.2018 / Edition 1 *Trade Paperback*
Book ID: ASAPCID2380745
ISBN: 978-1-946746-26-9
Library of Congress Cataloging-in-Publication Data

This book was published in the United States of America.
Great State of Michigan

Table of Contents

What a Way to Make A Living

by FRANKLIN R. JACKES

CHAPTER 1

WHAT A WAY TO MAKE A LIVING

My Granddaughter, Elisha gave me a beautiful blue scrapbook embossed with a metallic United States Air Force emblem. The scrapbook pages came with decorative aviation-oriented stickers and an assortment of appropriate page headings in patriotic colors and designs.

On the opening page, I have a newspaper clipping that evokes the title of <u>What a Way to Make a Living.</u> "Boy sizes up pilot's job, calls it pretty soft."

WASHINGTON-UPI

An unidentified third grade boy in California recently submitted an essay on why he wanted to fly an airplane when he grows up. His essay:

"I want to be an airline pilot because it's a fun job and easy to do. That is why there are so many pilots flying today."

Not much school!

"Pilots don't need much school. They just have to learn to read numbers so they can read instruments. I guess they should be able to read maps so they can find their way if they get lost.

"Pilots should be brave so they won't be scared if it's foggy and they can't see or if a wing or a motor falls off. They should stay calm so they'll know what to do,

"The salary pilots make is another thing I like. They make more money than they can spend. That is because most people think plane flying is dangerous except pilots don't because they know how easy it is.

Girls like pilots.

"There isn't much I don't like except that girls like pilots and all the stewardesses want to marry pilots so they always chase them away so they won't bother them.

"I hope I don't get airsick because I get car sick and I couldn't be a pilot and then I'd have to go to work."

The essay was reprinted in THE SHIELD, the United Airlines magazine for employees.

Growing up during WWII outside of St. Louis Mo, of

riding around on my bicycle (horse) with a cap gun (six shooter) and a cowboy hat until I was 12, I had not given any thought as to what I wanted to be, but I caught the flying urge at St. Louis Country Day School from 1948 until graduation in 1955.

The 56 acre campus was located about an hour's bus ride from my home in Ladue and just off the end of the runways of Lambert St. Louis International Airport. Day after day airliners, DC-3s, DC-4s Constellations, as well as Air National Guard and Naval Reserve aircraft, P-51s, F-4Us and others would take off to the SE and fly right over the school. When I could lean out the window from the last seat in the row in English class, I would hear better the sound of the engine(s) and know for sure just what type of airplane was passing over. This always elicited a response from Mr. Twitchell, "Okay, Birdman, back in the classroom."

Of course when McDonnell Douglas (McDonnell Aircraft then) started building the Banshee, Phantom and Voodoo it was hard to tell them apart without seeing them, and you had to look quickly to catch sight of a Voodoo. As usual, my classmates would ask, "Okay, Jackes, what kind is it?"

Since I had no idea what I wanted to do as far as college was concerned, my dad decided that I was going to stay in St. Louis and attend Washington University from which he had graduated at age 19 with a law degree in

1927. He felt that if it was good enough for him, it would be good enough for me.

With no idea of what to major in, I started out in a 5 year course in Architecture. During the "Indoctrination Week", before we Freshmen (and women) started classes, I met my future wife-the cutest, sweetest, most innocent little doll I had ever met. The first day of orientation camp, she said, "I'll bet you can't pronounce my name." I spelled KNUFINKE and pronounced it "Ka-new-finky". She must have been suitably impressed by that, even though she didn't pronounce mine correctly, because we started dating then and kept it up for four years.

When I joined a Fraternity; "Baby pink, Baby blue, I'm a Beta, Who are you?" she joined Delta Gamma. During the 1956 Presidential campaign, Sue was running for Homecoming Queen. Since I was sure she could win with a little publicity, I made up some fliers to hand out around the Quad Shop where there was a lot of traffic. The slogan said, "Some like Ike-finky, Some like Adlai-finky, but everybody likes Knufinke." She didn't win because her Sorority decided to back Jane Jones-(who could remember that name), because she was into more campus activities. I was happy that Ike-finky won anyway.

So, what to do with the rest of my life at age 18? I got out of Architecture School just before they kicked me out and transferred my major to "Jewish Engineering". With several engineering schools available at Washington University and 19% Jewish enrollment, everybody called Business School Jewish Engineering. However, my major became AFROTC.

What a way to make a living—not a living, since I wasn't being paid to drill at 7AM on Monday every week or wearing my uniform all over campus, but I did have many rewards thanks to Charlie Cain.

In 1958, Scott AFB had a T-28 for proficiency flying for rated officers within the local area of which Charlie was one. He and I had become student and teacher in the classroom as well as his tutorage with the newspaper that I published weekly in the Detachment on a mimeograph machine in purple ink.

Anyway, Charlie knew of my love of flying by then and he asked me if I wanted to go over to Scott AFB in Illinois and fly with him in the T-28. I eagerly accepted and found out for the first time about Flight Plans, Local Clearances, Weather Briefing, Radio Frequencies—things that would stay with me for years—especially in Pilot Training two years later. After takeoff, we cruised around the Scott AFB area. When Charlie pointed out a large estate below us with a moat around it, he told me that it belonged to Buster Wortmann, a notorious East Saint Louis gangster. As we were observing the fact that nobody could approach the island mansion without his knowledge and that he could drop the bridge on the only approach, Charlie poured the coals to the. T-28 and climbed straight up to 5-6000 feet. Just before the stall, we fell over on a wing and went into a spin right over the mansion. All I saw from the back seat was the spiraling ground, trees and the house until he pulled out of the spin and zoomed off into the training area. After that, all I remember was acrobatics and having to throw up in my flight cap. As we were taxiing in with the canopy back and fresh air cooling me off, I threw my messy flight cap out into the grass so I wouldn't have to admit to my airsickness. I didn't want it to get out to my fellow cadets who were jealous that I got to fly with Capt. Cain in the T-28. However, that fired me up with the ultimate desire to fly airplanes, even for a living if I could survive AFROTC.

CHAPTER 2

WHICH WASN'T EASY

I learned quite a few things in ROTC besides how to drill on Monday morning at 0700 before class down on the drill field all the way down the East edge of the Washington University campus—a pretty good march in itself. I learned to publish a Detachment newspaper that had to be typed, edited and run off on a mimeograph machine with purple ink and stinky paper—what a mess every week!

My most profound lesson was with respect to race relations in the early 50's both in St. Louis and in the US Air Force.

When the Detachment was organizing a picnic for all cadets during our junior year, the father of the cadet who was in charge of the picnic's location told his son that no Negros would be allowed in his park, the park where the picnic was scheduled to be held. Since we only had one Negro in the whole Detachment, two or three of us decided that for the good of the majority, we would explain the situation to the individual and make it up to him at a later date. Thinking we had solved a minor problem, I was surprised to be called on the carpet by the Professor of Air Science(PAS). The Lt. Col. told me that the picnic had been cancelled and then asked me if I knew what the Air Force's policy was on Integration vs Segregation. I had to admit that I knew there was no policy on Segregation and that Integration was the Government's policy—which I had violated and might have severe consequences.

Somehow, I managed to survive dismissal from the program and even hung on through another "carpet-calling" episode during which my father promised he would sell my 55 Studebaker Commander after I had received a speeding ticket. I had been trying to return my four year sweetheart Sue back to the dorm before curfew. With that assurance of his attempt to keep me in AFROTC, my father did indeed sell my car and the PAS kept me in the Corps.

Between our sophomore year and our junior year, we were to be subjected to an indoctrination program called Pre-Summer Training Unit, or PSTU. It was designed to prepare us for our Summer Training at an Air Force Base that conducted Pilot Training. In order to prepare us who were going on to Flight Training, the seniors of the Detachment took us over to Scott AFB in the middle of summer to participate in a fraternity-type hazing program of indoctrination to life as a pilot trainee. It was very similar in intensity to Hell Week at Beta Theta Pi when I was a Freshman in the fact that we were required to jump to every order given by our "leaders" from the time we got off the bus to the end of the ordeal on Sunday afternoon—a really long weekend. It was "Fall in, Dress Right Dress, Forward March"—on and on until it was time to upgrade our barracks to livable standards, according to our senior tormentors. Due to the fact that those old yellow, two story barracks on the very east side of the base hadn't been inhabited for two or three years, our work was cut out for us, to say the least. First, we had to sweep, mop, wash and scrub just to try to return these old quarters to livable conditions, not to mention to the level of our leader's white-glove inspection standards. Since some of us were billeted upstairs and the other half of our flight was to occupy the space below, our chore was burdened by the fact that we had to carry mops and buckets full of soapy water up the stairs in order to properly mop the old wooden floors before we tackled the stairway itself. My idea was not the best—to empty the buckets of soapy water down the floor and then swing our mops from one end to the other.

My fraternity brother, Ike, was in the flight downstairs, and as we sluiced the water over the dirty floor, we heard a pair of boots pounding up the stairwell. It seemed that the flight below had just finished their cleaning to the satisfaction of the powers that be, and had begun to make their bunks with clean linen. When we sloshed the soapy water on our upstairs floor, most of it poured through the floor and deluged down below after flowing over the dirty, dusty, heating vents in the first floor ceiling, thereby raining muddy water all over the clean half-made bunks below. Ike was livid, to say the least, and we were no longer friends even though we were still fraternity brothers.

Our Training Officer always looked sharp, creased, and polished. One of their secrets that they eventually revealed to us neophytes was the trick of cutting down suspenders, sewing them together and attaching one end

9

to the top of their socks and the other end to their shirt tails. It kept their shirt tails permanently tucked in much to the consternation of us "plebes".

Along with the normal marching "Column Right, By the Left Flank, To the Rear, Harch" and all the other sweaty marching maneuvers, we were required to defend a tennis court from invasion. In order to do this, we had to form a circle, arm-in-arm and call out, "The British Are Coming, The British Are Coming!" Just another silly part of PSTU, but in two years, it would be our turn to "haze" the new guys was during the summer of 1957, before my junior year of ROTC. We had already been indoctrinated in some of the fundamentals of Basic Training during our Pre-STU at Scott AFB, so we knew about sweat and strain in the summer heat.

We were flown down to Vance AFB in Enid Oklahoma in a Missouri ANG C-47 out of St. Louis Lambert International. (Little did I know how much more time I would spend in a Gooney Bird during the next 15 years or so. I remember that I wasn't too impressed with the "tail-draggin' trash hauler" because it wasn't a fighter plane like the ones I had listened to and watched during my high school years from '51-'55.

Here at Vance AFB we learned more about military protocol. One thing I learned rather harshly from the Aerodrome Officer of the Day, to whom we were assigned to follow around during his duty shift, was, "Close enough for Government Work" was a no-no. I was lectured about how important government work is and how, if you are doing government work, it should be done well and by the regulations. "If it's not worth doing well, it's not worth doing at all."

We also were treated to our first jet ride in a T-33. Hardly any of us ROTC cadets survived the heat, sweat and "losing one's lunch" that was SOP for the cadet's orientation to the world of flight at 20,000 ft. above the Earth. However, it did serve to whet the appetite-not for replacement food, but for flying itself.

We were introduced to the "idiot box"-a ground-fixed torture machine that was supposed to imitate flying but never very well. The LINK TRAINER merely showed us what lay ahead for those of us who would eventually attend pilot training.

The greatest benefit of ROTC in the 50's in St. Louis was FIP Flight Indoctrination Program—which the US Government was financing to see if third year cadets were going to be suitable for Pilot Training in two years. Evidently, the thinking was why not find out with a relatively inexpensive light aircraft experience rather than finding out after Pre-Flight and six months of Primary Pilot Training.

Having participated in the Ground Observer Program and received a "personal" letter signed by none other than Dwight D. Eisenhower, I had seen how Air Traffic Control (ATC) follows all aircraft in the US and how important radio communication is to pilots and ground controllers.

Now I was going to find out what no-radio, local, low altitude, uncontrolled VFR (Visual Flight Rules) flying was all about. Even though FIP eventually lead to a private pilot's license, it was minimally funded. Therefore, in the Spring of 1954, my introduction to the world of aviation consisted of daily excursions out to a small airport in Fenton, Missouri alongside the Merrimack River long before the Chrysler plant was built nearby and the highway through the area wasn't yet Interstate 44.

Day 1 of the Flight Indoctrination Program consisted of a thorough examination of our 750 pound sewing machine with wings on it—a Piper PA-11, a four cylinder 65HP Lycoming engine, yellow fabric covered tail dragger that supposedly get me and my 6'2" 200lb instructor airborne. "Up in the air, junior birdman" was the sneering motto of all my fraternity brothers and of course anybody in Army ROTC.

After much discussion about LIFT, drag, Power-to-Weight Ratio, Power, Thrust—"Get on with it!" we finally came to the point where we actually climbed into the airplane and actually fired up the engine. Now, we were getting somewhere. With a mighty roar of the "Bug-Smasher's" engine, we finally lurched forward to the take-off end of the 4500 foot asphalt and gravel runway. FINALLY!

I was allowed to make the take-off from the front seat with my instructor's feet on my rudder pedals from the back seat. Throttle to max, stick, neutral, brakes off, lift off at 60mph and climb at 65, left turn out after passing the end of the runway—Yada, Yada, Yada—Look Ma, I'm Flying! Grass, trees, river, fields below me! What a thrill! The first of many thrills of leaving the ground and rising above everything around you—only those who have experienced it in a light airplane know what it is like. After throttling back to Climb Power up over the river on downwind leg, we headed out over the fields and trees to the practice area where it was my turn to follow through for turns, climbs and descents, stalls and steep turns. One of these involved a 90° degree bank turn with power up and increasing back pressure on the stick until the aircraft swaps sides and you're now going around the opposite way. It's called a 720 stall and it's really fun to do.

Now comes the real exciting part of flying—coming back down to the ground. The proper way is to make sure that the main gear and the tail wheel touch down at the same time, thereby assuring that the airplane is in a stall, called a three-point landing. But to do it is not easy at first and takes a lot of practice. Too fast and you bounce, too slow and you fall with a sickening thud. There is a very fine line between throttle, stick, airspeed, altitude, approach angle, wind, attitude, obstacles, ground surface—on and on and on, so by the time you have practiced enough to please the GIB (Guy in Back), you're ready to SOLO. Now here is the defining moment in any would-be pilot's life, let alone his career. The instructor merely has you taxi back for another take-off, then, somewhere near the ramp area, he suddenly applies the brakes and jumps out—leaving you feeling a bit lonely but excited. This is it! Sink or swim. Do it or screw it-whatever! So I taxied out, checked final approach to make sure nobody was going to land on top of me, and pushing the little throttle knob all the way forward, started down the runway all by myself. Everything was going great until on downwind leg over the river, suddenly the split side door sprang open and scared me to a panic. However, I managed to keep my concentration on actually flying the airplane, turning base leg, again looking out for final approach traffic, reducing power, and establishing a decent descent on final approach. By this time I figured the open door was no biggie, and let go of it as I got ready for landing. In the PA-11, there's not much to do to get ready for landing except stare at the point where you want to stop flying and watch the airspeed indicator. No gear down, flaps down, radio call—pretty easy. After I bumped into the ground without bouncing into the air again, I was so relieved I almost "relieved" myself, but managed to take off again and prove two more times that the first landing wasn't luck or a fluke. There is a great truth about flying— "A good landing is one you can walk away from, but a great landing is one that allows you to use the airplane the next day."

I was certainly through flying for that day, except for my euphoria of having soloed. However, there were still some 30 hours more I needed to complete the program and receive a pilot's license. These included 2 to 4 hours of instrument time which called for an aircraft with a little more sophistication than the yellow "tail dragger". Now I was going to fly a Piper Tri-Pacer, a tricycle gear with more power and some radios and NAVAIDS, at least a VOR and an ADF. I was introduced to the mysterious world of Instrument Flying—to radials, bearings and the difference between the two, holding a course after intercepting the required one, station passage, outbound course—a whole new dimension, not just airspeed, altitude, turn and slip and fuel gauge, but without even looking outside the cockpit, knowing just where you are and how to go from there to where you want to land. Not yet ILS or Ground Controlled Approach (GCA), although I think we did one in the T-28 at Scott AFB, but I had no idea what that was all about, just my stinky flight cap. At least, I knew how to intercept a desired bearing or radial and follow it to the airfield where I wanted to land visually.

One idiosyncrasy of the Tri-Pacer was that it had doors like a car on each side and the static port that sensed atmospheric pressure was on the right side of the fuselage aft of the door. One of my instructor's tricks was to have the student concentrating on holding a course at an exact altitude. Then he would open the door on his side. Not only would the airplane turn to the right, the airspeed and altitude indicators would jump up and down with the disturbed airflow over the static port. It would definitely get the student's attention.

One morning I called out to the field to see how the weather was out in Fenton. My instructor said he could see 4 or 5 ducks heading south, but they were walking. Then one bright and relatively smooth day we took off on a "dual ride" and he said, "Take it up to 10,000 feet." I didn't think that little 65hp machine would make it up that high, but after 35 or 40 minutes, we staggered up to 12 O'clock on the Altimeter. Suddenly, he closed the throttle and said, "Forced landing!" Well, one of the first things a pilot is supposed to do when the engine quits is look for a place to land in an emergency. But, from 10,000 feet, the situation doesn't seem too threatening. By clearing the engine occasionally and applying a bit of carburetor heat to keep it from freezing up, I managed to keep the engine from actually quitting so we could make a missed approach from the landing area I had picked out. After about 15 minutes of cigarette smoking and idle chatter about what could cause engine failure, he asked me, "Where are you going to put this thing?" By now we were below 1000 feet and I had to find a field in a hurry. I don't know if I could have actually force-landed in the only field reachable in the last minute of our simulated emergency, but when I was told to go missed approach and poured the coals to the little Lycoming and started to climb back to the direction of home plate, I was looking up at a highway underpass and I wasn't going to fly under it. I nursed it up a couple of hundred feet and skimmed right over Interstate 44. No driver under us could have been scared more than I was. It personified the phrase: "Hours and hours of boredom, punctuated by moments of stark terror!" Although I had not heard the term before that, I had become a perfect example of "loss of situational awareness". Some fighter pilots in combat would become non-living examples of loss of situational awareness—not knowing where you are and where the sun, ground ack-ack guns and enemy fighters are as well as wingmen, tankers and friendly territory are. It was a valuable lesson learned early in my flying career.

CHAPTER 3

OFF WE GO INTO THE WILD

Being now a 2nd Lt with a BSBA, a private pilot's license and a brand new Studebaker Silver Hawk, I was on my way to a fun-filled summer, back and forth between St. Louis County and Granite City Illinois until August 15th when Sue and I were married. After a honeymoon at the Greenbriar in White Sulpher Springs W. Virginia, we took our orders to Pre-flight Training and all our wedding presents and acquired possessions in a 4x6 U-Haul and headed down the road to Lackland AFB in San Antonio TX for the beginning of our Air Force life together. I loved my Studebaker Silver Hawk with its 3-speed manual transmission and overdrive in all three gears, but the 4x6 U-Haul on our trailer hitch degraded not only the performance of the 152hp engine, but didn't do our gas mileage any good either. Somewhere in the middle of Arkansas, we came to a small town with one stoplight. Unfortunately for our overloaded not-so-hot rod the stoplight was at the bottom of a long rather steep hill, followed by an equally long and steep up-hill out of town. I never made it to a stop at the bottom with my brakes smoking and then had to drag our clothes, dishes, pots and pans up to the top and back to level ground and on to San Antonio.

Once we arrived at Lackland AFB, we were billeted in Billy Mitchell Village where 3 or 4 thousand couples had set up housekeeping previously. It was August in Texas and we had no air conditioning. While I was being fitted for a myriad of uniforms, drilling from classroom to mess hall to athletic fields and sweating off any excess pounds that newly married life had put on, my bride of three weeks was trying to establish a semblance of home life. On our first Saturday, she fixed scrambled eggs in our brand new electric skillet, one of our wedding gifts. Since it had never been used before, and was stainless steel, the eggs came out a moldy green color and sent her into a crying jag that lasted all weekend. But the weather cooled off, the cooking became better and with a full complement of uniforms, including shorts, blues, silver tans, (but no "horse blanket" overcoat) it was time for our next set of orders to Primary Pilot Training.

When we weren't marching, attending class or having our uniforms fitted, we actually had time to enjoy one of the base's recreation facilities, namely, the golf course. I had a set of old golf clubs somewhere in our limited household goods, so I dug them out and headed for the clubhouse. Before I teed off on No. 1, already steaming in early September in San Antonio Texas, I was warned about always carrying an iron with me whenever I went into the rough, as a weapon—something about rattlesnakes. The most challenging hole was a par-5 dog-leg to the right about 525 yards long. If you could hit your tee shot across the corner, the ball would hit on the rock-hard fairway and roll downhill toward the green. The 2nd shot was only a 9-iron or wedge to the pin. However, if your shot was short you had to go into the long brown grass, equipped with your trusty 5-iron and look for your ball, being careful to walk slowly and heavily. I only played it twice, once I made it across the corner, played a nine to the green and two-putted for a birdie. The other time I hit short of the dog-leg and dropped one on the edge for my third and took a 6.

In Louisiana, at England AFB, there was a sign on the golf course, by a low, usually wet hazard, that read: "BEWARE OF SNAKES AND ALLIGATORS". Fortunately, I never hit a ball in there, but I was certainly "AWARE". Since we were both from the St. Louis area, our assignment to Malden AB in the Missouri boot heel was a welcome outcome for us. It was a different story for all the others who received the same orders. Nobody else, except Dan Hostettler wanted Malden, so a game of "Switch" was in full progress-not with me, but all around me.

There was a good reason Dan Hostettler didn't want to exchange Malden for Barstow, Spence or Bainbridge, all in the Deep South. Dan and his wife were from Campbell Mo., about 15 minutes from Malden. When they received their travel pay for their PCS move, the check was for $.96--12 cents a mile for 8 miles. One of the other "drawbacks" of the program at Malden was the fact that it was the only primary school still flying two prop planes, the T-34 and the T-28. The others were checking out in the T-37, a 6,000 lb "dog whistle" with two jet engines.

When we finally arrived at Malden Mo., we found a

cadre of military officers and a few enlisted men, but all civilian instructors working for Anderson Flight School and well qualified to teach us "brown bars" a thing or two about the world of military aviation. If not, the military check pilots certainly could. We were divided into 4-man units, each with a civilian instructor. We drew flight gear, including an E-6B "whiz wheel" and began our daily school routine of weather, aerodynamics, aircraft engines and systems, performance graphs and checklists with emergency procedures to memorize to go with our Dash-1s, the T-34 Flight Manual, that if read long enough and well enough would teach a fledgling pilot everything he would need to know about flying the shiny, sleek fast and aerobatic T-34. BUT! When were we going to get to actually fly this non-jet marvel?

One aspiring military aviator actually showed up at his Primary Pilot Training Base with his own T-28. Of course he didn't get to fly it any more, other than to hump it over to Poplar Bluff and park it there for 6 months while he learned a new way to fly it—the military way. The school almost washed him out because he had so many bad habits from flying it his way, but I don't remember if they did or not. I know we never saw that silver T-28 with the blue lightning stripe along the side ever again.

Finally, the day came when each of us received our "Dollar Ride". After our very thorough instructional pre-flight with our checklists firmly in hand, we were each allowed to climb up on the wing, dragging our bulky and heavy parachutes bumping along behind us, up into the front cockpit where we found that our parachute was also our seat cushion. Now, staring at the instrument panel before our very eyes, not as a picture/diagram in our Dash-1s, we began with our Before Starting Engine checklist, the first of probably 1000+ in my 14 ½ year flying career.

My first instructor was, to me at 21, an ancient aviator who probably had more flying time than I would ever have in my lifetime if I lived as long as he had. He had a gruff, raspy voice and a nasty habit of smoking cigars in the back seat. By the time we arrived at the end of the runway ready for takeoff, I wasn't sure I had done anything right to that point. After we received takeoff clearance, he said, "All right, you make the takeoff." Here it comes, the most thrilling moment of my life! Not a rumbling noisy, bumpy takeoff in a 65hp kite, but the smooth acceleration from 225hp from 0 to 65 knots, nose wheel off, main gear off at 85, gear up and climb at 95—you have to feel it to understand the exhilaration it gives you when the ground breaks away, your shadow gets smaller racing along over the ground, the trees are below you, the town is spread out below you and the road out of Malden can be seen as a black line all the way to Dexter. Hills aren't above you anymore and the clouds are coming down to meet you—can I go through them? Of course, the reality of the fact that the GIB (Guy in Back) is actually flying the airplane brings you back to Earth since this is only your "Dollar Ride", but still, you have "slipped the surly bonds of Earth" and now you have to undergo the rigors of a "madman" in the back seat who is going to find out if you are cut out to be a pilot worthy of his attention and expertise. Since one way to find out is to perform a series of acrobatic maneuvers, especially while smoking a cigar in the back seat, Mr. Summers only found out that that didn't agree with my stomach and equilibrium, not that it would keep me from achieving my goal of becoming an Air Force pilot. The cure for air-sickness is to fly the airplane yourself. After my "Dollar Ride" the next dual missions consisted of my flying and him kibbitzing from behind. After about 8 hours of attaining a certain degree of proficiency, the magic moment of "Taxi back—I'll get out" came and it was time for my second solo. Since the T-34 is such a sweetheart to fly, I made my required 3 traffic pattern laps with two touch-and-goes, affectionately known as TAGs, without any mishaps, forgotten gear down calls, missing flap settings or radio calls to the "Tweety" control in the RSU (Runway Supervisory Unit) at the side of the runway. Even touchdowns were fairly smooth, stay on the centerline, flaps up, Mixture still Rich, Prop still Max RPM, Throttle Max and off we go again into the "wild blue yonder". Boy! I really loved flying that airplane! This was a big step up from my PA-11 with radios, retractable landing gear, flaps and variable pitch prop.

Now came the day that I was to transition into the T-28—that tall, ugly, noisy, complicated 800 horsepower brute. The last words of advice from my gravel-voiced GIB were, "Now, remember, Jackes, every time you fly the T-28, take a bite out of it."

Well, I don't know if I ever bit a piece out of it, but I learned not to be scared of it and to like it even more than the T-34. First off, the only way to enter the cockpit was to stand next to the left side behind the wing and, dragging your seat pack parachute behind you, mount the two steps cleverly built into the lowered flap—hence one of the last items on the Engine Shutdown Checklist: Flaps—Check Full Down—otherwise you couldn't get off without jumping 5 or

6 feet to the asphalt and nobody else could get into the cockpit.

Another idiosyncrasy of the "Maytag Messerschmitt" was when you reached the cockpit, sitting on your seat pack parachute, the canopy rail was even with your hips and the instrument panel was a tall, wide maze of dials and gauges almost up to your upper lip. Once you were settled into this "open-air" office you had many more checklist items with which to contend, including Engine Start.

The engine on the T-28 of Primary Pilot Training was a Kaiser built and modified mill with 800HP in 7 cylinders, twin stacks, which gave it an alternating roar—3 on one side and 4 on the other. With a 10ft two-bladed prop it required 10 blade rotations with the Starter, Primer Button, Magneto Switch ON and the Throttle out of Idle Detent to about 3" travel. If done correctly in the proper sequence, the monster radial would come to life with much smoke behind and an occasional backfire, or blow-back. The first three of these operations were accomplished with the right hand on the lower right corner of the instrument panel. The Starter and Primer were easily reached with two fingers, but the Mag Switch had to be shoved right with the forefinger or thumb. It took a while to master the technique, but eventually everyone did or they didn't fly.

Now, getting the beast into the air was the next fact of life in the effort to become an aviator. It was said of the T-28, like so many prop-driven airplanes before it like the Sopwith Camel, the SPAD, P-40 P-51 especially, that takeoff was "a sudden application of power designed to get you airborne before torque pulled you off the left side of the runway." Since that big 10ft prop turning at 2800 RPM from right to left caused centrifugal force want to make the airframe follow that motion to the left. As I recall, you had to dial in 5° degrees of right rudder trim just to help keep the nose wheel somewhere near the centerline. It was also said that one could always tell a T-28 pilot—a great big right leg and a little skinny left leg.

But once you got that beauty in the air, you had a tiger-by-the-tail, that's why the "Tweety" Runways were on the inside for the T-34s and the "Tiger" Runways were on the outside for the T-28s. The RSUs were Tweety Control and Tiger Control. The Instructors manned them on rotating shifts and graded landings and checked to assure nobody landed gear-up or no-flap. On one occasion, Tommy Wright, the Senior Pilot among the school staff, told a T-28 student to go around due to another airplane on the runway. When the student applied go-around power, the engine froze and the big, heavy prop sheared from the crankshaft, embedding itself in the macadam runway. Even with no power, the gear down and the loss of all that weight from the nose, the student managed to land perfectly without anyone having time to give any word of advice. Tommy Wright said if anyone had said anything, he probably would have screwed up the landing. None of us wanted to be the next student pilot to have to go around.

Now it was time for night flying. Our class book for 61-Charlie class has a quip in it that says; "Night came in— chip detector light came on." The old Kaiser engine in the T-28 had many differences from the T-34 and its rather mundane 225HP 6 cylinder horizontally opposed

Continental smoothie. The 800HP radial with its alternating exhaust in the collector ring was not a smooth performer. It had cowl flaps to aid in cooling and they were wide open on the ground. Also incorporated into this engineering marvel was a magnetic plug inserted in the oil sump to detect metal shavings in the oil system. When they collected in the sump they closed a circuit to a red light prominently located on the instrument panel. When that light came on, you had better be ready to land. One student had it come on at the top of a loop. When he bottomed out the field was in sight and he landed with an emergency. Right after touchdown the engine stopped and he had to be towed off the runway. Every student added that to the list of things not desirable—like go-arounds.

Back to night flying and the preparation for our night cross country flight. As with the day cross country before, we had to do all of our mission planning the day before. One had to have every NAVAID, checkpoint, estimated time to each one along the way, altitude, airspeed, wind component which affected groundspeed, fuel remaining at each point along the entire 2 ½ hour route through Southern Illinois, Kentucky, across the Mississippi River into Arkansas and back to good old Malden. None of us had had much trouble navigating along our mapped route in the relatively clear daylight hours. But, even after a couple of night locals, we were deemed ready to soar off into the dark and grope our way around the cross-country trek by ourselves. That makes for a scary 2 ½ hours with the cockpit lights turned down, a red flashlight trained on the Route Card, map, checklist, stick, throttle, prop, mixture fuel control lever, engine instruments, Manifold Pressure and

RPM, ADF, VOR, UHF radio, position reports—and what lights are those? Is that Memphis, where's Blytheville? Can't tell where the River is at night. Which highway is that? Now we hear Dean Heal call; "I don't know where I am! I'm over a large city—I think it's Memphis!" "Just orbit to the left and turn on your landing lights," came the reply. "We'll come and get you." So some Instructor went and found him and dragged him back on the route to the next checkpoint. I'll be darned if he didn't get lost again. The next time he was found, he just followed the leader back to Malden.

Everybody had to call Ops when he returned from night flying or else it cost him a case of beer. Following my night cross country, I was one of the last ones to return to the ramp. I was so relieved to have accomplished that ordeal, I forgot to "Ramp out" with Ops. Since I had already shut down the Mighty Kaiser, I was going to have to restart the engine so I could call in. No problem—it was dark, late and would only take a minute. I hit the starter, primer, mag switch sequence per checklist, not realizing that I didn't need the primer, and got everybody's attention when the fuel hit the hot cylinders and collection ring. As soon as I touched the throttle, fireballs started erupting from both stacks and cannonballed down the ramp behind me where 15 or 20 T-28s were parked. Needless to say, I had announced the fact that I had forgotten to Ramp Out. It cost me a case of beer plus a lot of humiliation.

After night flying, came Instruments. This part of the curriculum followed weeks of Link training and orientation in a tiny box that supposedly simulated actual flight. When we started flying the first take off was made by the student in the back seat "under the hood". The hood was a flexible, silver coated cover that pulled forward from the rear and hooked to the rear instrument panel so that the student couldn't see anything outside the cockpit—just the instrument panel and all the gauges—Manifold Pressure, RPM, Airspeed Indicator, Heading indicator, Altimeter, Climb and Descent needle, Turn and Slip plus NAVAIDS and controls. So, here you are, lined up on the takeoff runway, under the hood, and Neil Burke, my Instructor says; "You got it, make the takeoff, turn to (heading), climb to (altitude) and track outbound on (bearing) to---"SURE! You talk about pressure—and not just manifold pressure. Throttle max, right rudder to hold runway heading, airspeed to 65, nose gear off and climb, gear up when climb indicator indicates positive rate of climb and you reach 300 feet, climb power from 38" and 2800RPM to 36" and 2400RPM, flaps up, turn to heading and begin outbound track interception. Climb to 3500 feet, Level off, hold heading on outbound track, hold altitude and reduce power to cruise and call for Cruise Checklist—all that in about 4 or 5 minutes. Of course the instructor is with you all the way, but he is also grading you on all the little errors you made on airspeed, heading, altitude and procedures during the whole departure. If you passed all that, you began learning how to fly "aural-null" procedures. It takes about 12 pages in AFM51-37, Instrument Flying, so the explanation is too long to discuss, and no one has flown "aural-null" since 1962 when the old Adcock Ranges were decommissioned and we had fully automated Automatic Direction Finding capability. However, we were required to learn such an antiquated procedure in case we ever became lost with nothing but a commercial radio station to home in on and were completely socked in.

One day, we were in the Instrument Training Area with Neil in the front seat and I under the hood in the back following orders to track such and such a bearing, intercept and hold, etc., etc. when, after a half an hour, I started to receive heading corrections of 2° or 3° degrees and altitude corrections of 5 to 10 feet along with airspeed changes of 2 to 3 knots. After 5 or 10 minutes of this goofiness, he said; "You can come out from under the hood now—I got it." I was very relieved from the tension until I looked to my left and saw a T-28 five feet away and slightly ahead. I almost jumped out of my boots to think I'd been flying formation without ever seeing the other airplane! That's how goofy Neil Burke was. He very seldom smiled, except, I thought, when I took his picture sitting in the cockpit of a T-28 and I stood on the wing to snap a shot before graduation. I could have sworn he was smiling when I took the picture, but when it came out, he wasn't smiling—just his Frankenstein scowl.

One of our (Sue and I) memorable events from Malden life was night-flying when we were trying to watch 1960's TV beneath the traffic pattern that came close to our little duplex with a small, portable black and white TV set with "rabbit ears" for an antenna. Every time a T-28 came over in the "Tiger" traffic pattern, the picture would go "toes-up". In addition to that, the landlady had decided to raise the rent from $70 monthly to $75 a month. Sue and I drove down to Kennett, the County Seat of Dunklin County, to confront this heartless landlady who wanted to charge us an additional $5 a month with only two months left on our tour. We found her in a wheel chair and "brow-beat" that poor woman into waiting until April to raise the rent when we would be on our way to our next assignment. An interesting sidelight to that story is the fact that, in 1960 we were paying $70 a month rent while earning only $410 a month as a 2nd Lt on flying status. Forty-four years later, at a Malden reunion, I met a lady outside the VFW hall where we were having our reunion dinner. I mentioned that I had found the old duplex for which I had paid $70 a month rent. She then told me; "I live there now and I pay $410 a month rent." What a surprise! Of course in 1960, gasoline was only 28 cents a gallon, ground beef was 33 cents a pound (for our Hamburger Helper). On Saturdays I used to go to town by myself and visit a local bar where a glass of draught beer was only 15 cents. The local farmers would come in there and buy a can of tomato juice for 20 cents and mix it with a 15 cent beer and call it a Bloody Mary. For two dollars, they could drink all day. Life in the Boot Heel was good, even if the weather wasn't always great. One event was the arrival of a dust storm which was spawned by the passage of a rather deep low associated with a cold front and the fact that all the fields of cotton surrounding Malden were fallow. By the time the weather-guessers had realized that we were in for a "bit of a blow", the leading edge of the storm was within sight of the traffic pattern. We were immediately ordered to head for the field and land ASAP. By the time all the airplanes were safely on the ground, the dust was already blowing and we were all glad not to be flying in it because the visibility dropped to 100 feet and everything was being covered with dust. The next day, Sue or I was taking a bath—no shower available—and the grit in the tub was like sandpaper. We vacuumed and dusted for days trying to get rid of the stuff that had accumulated in every corner and on every surface.

The other memorable event was a 10" snowstorm. We had experienced some snow on the ground and what it did for landmark recognition, but we hadn't lived through having to find the T-28s on the ramp covered with inches of snow which had to be swept off all surfaces before we could even mount the wing or having to pound the wheel chocks out from under the main gear with fire bottles. Our class book has a great picture of Gary Mohler sweeping the snow off the wing of his T-28 as well as a beautiful snow woman with a mop for a hairdo.

Of course, no history of our tour of duty at Malden would be complete without the tale of the "Horse blanket Caper". As the class before us was to graduate and we were to form up in ranks with dress blues for the graduation Parade in Review, we were informed that the uniform of the day would include the mandatory "horse blanket"—a blue wool overcoat that all enlisted men had been issued, but that student officers had not. We were supposed to include that item of our military wardrobe in our initial inventory that we purchased at Lackland AFB back in August, when it was 95° degrees and we were more inclined to have purchased walking shorts and long socks than a bulky blue overcoat. Since this seemed to be a universal oversight by all of us who had to attend the parade in 30° degree weather, we were mystified as to how we were going to solve this dilemma. Fortunately, the wife of our First Lieutenant next door neighbor, knew that the Base Exchange at Blytheville AFB had a stock of them as well as Clothing Sales. Therefore, she collected the required funds from each of us and bought both venues out of blue wool overcoats, never to be worn by any of us evermore. Again, our class book had another quip to the effect that the uniform of the day was; Socks, Jocks and Sombreros. That's fine as long as the snow isn't above the tops of your knee socks.

I had always liked to draw, particularly airplanes, so I was able to create some rather clever cartoons for our 61-Charlie class book, which resides in the Malden historical museum to this day. One of the cartoons showed a T-28 going straight up, student in the rear under the "hood" and captioned: "And recover with the nose slightly below the horizon".

Since we'd been content to accept the assignment to Malden, we didn't have far to go to drive up to St. Louis and Granite City for Christmas vacation. This was long before Interstate 55 ran north/south up the Mississippi River to St. Louis, so we had to take old US61/67, the 2-lane highway from Sikeston and through Cape Girardeau. However, we decided to cross the "Big Muddy" at Tiptonville. We drove our '59 Studebaker Silver Hawk as far as Cape Girardeau, Mo. and stopped for the night. We found one of the oldest hotels west of the Mississippi in an ancient opera house. The three-story black building had not only a hotel in it but a charming first floor restaurant with a large brick fireplace and a marvelously accommodating elderly black waiter. We were happy to get off the cold, slightly snowy highway and even happier to find sanctuary in the red, gold and dark wood dining room without any other diners. Our waiter cheerfully brought us draught Budweiser, Caesar salad, prime rib and even dessert until we felt full, warm, buzzed and like one of the family.

After a soothing night's rest, we headed for the Illinois side of the River. Our next hurdle was the Tiptonville Ferry. We drove to the ancient road sign indicating the road to the ferry and followed its rutted path to the landing on the river bank. It looked like something out of Huckleberry Finn, a raft/cattle barge that was only big enough to haul 4 cars and since we were the only car intending to cross, we had the "River Queen" all to ourselves. After a half an hour of chugging at a 20 degree angle up stream to keep the current from docking us in Vicksburg, we arrived on the Illinois side. From there it was about 3 hours through the winter countryside to home and our first Christmas.

When we returned to good old Malden, we were half way through our tour with nothing to do but finish the Primary Pilot Training Program. The saying there was that the population didn't change much in Malden because every time a kid was born, some guy left town. Of course, the opposite was also professed among the locals, that every time the train went through at 0430, it was too early to get up so there was only one other thing to do.

My wife Sue taught school as a substitute for 3 or 4 months in the Dunklin County School. All of the kids wore bib overalls, few had coats and only about half even had shoes. The school was a large brick building with nothing but a wrought iron fence around it and no grass—just dirt. It's not easy to teach kids under those conditions. This was what we heard was the greatest cotton-producing area in the Country.

Now it was time to relocate from there to the "other" greatest cotton-producing area in the Country,

Lubbock Texas, Reese AFB. Now, on to the next step in my formal pilot training curriculum. My AF Form 475, TRAINING REPORT, came along with me. Dated 23 April 1960, it described my Primary Pilot Training record as: 130 ½ hours of student performance: "Lt. Jackes is a typically average young officer. Attitude and motivation are slightly below average----". What a way to start my flying career—average leadership capabilities. Hopefully, I could overcome such "average performance" in the next 6 months. On to jets (T-33) and a decent assignment afterwards.

Having had one ride in a T-33 at Vance AFB in Enid Oklahoma in 1958 as part of my Summer Training Unit during AFROTC training program for pilot-eligible cadets, I found the smooth power and speed of the T-33 an exciting change from the "Maytag Messerschmitt" and the limits of 10,000 'and 180 knots. The first ride was so exhilarating—to take off so fast and smoothly, climb at 240 knots to 25,000'-30,000', chase clouds, do rolls and loops with such ease, it seemed so routine that I felt that I could ace this part of the course.

Then I found out that it wasn't as easy as it seemed once I was in control. My Instructor was a 1st Lt. named John Gardner. He was a cool, laid-back dude who had come from B-25s to become a jet instructor. He was a very entertaining story-teller as well as a smooth pilot and womanizer. His motto on Friday nights was, "Eatin's cheatin'." During the week he would clean me out at Liar's Dice at the O. Club bar, but on Friday night he was off to Lubbock to the local drive-in. Lubbock was in a dry county. If you wanted to buy liquor or beer, you either bought it tax-free on base to be consumed there, or pay the tax to consume it off-base. But if you wanted the "Good Stuff", you went to the drive-in (Night Owl #3), drove around once, held up the number of fingers for how many you wanted, drove around the second time to assure your order was received. On the third orbit, you exchanged the proper remuneration for the merchandise you ordered. The nearest bar outside of the O. Club was in Post, TX, 40 miles down the road.

For us, Friday nights were not for studying and early bed time. They were spent at the O. Club. A very lively place with lots of student pilots discussing, what else—flying maneuvers, with all the hand gestures attendant thereto. I was hooked on Liar's Dice, a very popular bar game. With 5 dice under the cup, you could call any poker hand you thought you could bluff your opponent into believing. You only lost when you didn't have what you claimed under the cup and were called. There is a lot of strategy to the game, but lying is a big part of one's success. My sweet, innocent wife, Sue, after learning how to play from John, became so good at it that she won almost every game. Everybody believed her with her sweet, innocent smile. Eventually, I quit playing with her.

Learning to fly the sleek, quiet, smooth T-33 and not have to worry about mixture, prop, throttle, cowl flaps, over boost and chip detectors was a soothing change, but soon we were to learn about flying at three times the speed and altitude. Also new was formation-flying. That was truly scary but exhilarating. The first time we did a pitchout and rejoin I thought I would get the hang out of this "close-order drill" at 300 knots at 20,000'. Then I realized, as Zeke-4, the last man in the formation, that I was looking up at the ground and there were 3 T-33s below me. That will get the adrenalin flowing during a formation barrel roll. During a 4-ship loop when you're the last one in trail, you must reduce power slightly going up and add power slightly going down because the first airplanes start slowing down before you going up and start picking up speed before you on the earthbound portion of the maneuver.

Our cross-country in the jet was a two day affair, going first to Biloxi Mississippi where John had taught foreign students to fly the T-33 and who still had friends stationed there. After landing at Keesler AFB, we checked into the BOQ, showered and shaved, and, while I was getting ready to go to the O. Club and have a few, John said he was going to a couple of joints off-base and that I could join him if I could find him. After I had my fill of beer and burgers, I was back at the BOQ room when John came in rather noisily looking for money. He said he had three women who wanted to have a drinking party, so I told him to take what I had on the dresser and off he went. Six hours later, we were filed and ready to depart. We had to hurry before the temperature rose above 83-85 degrees due to the short runway and degraded performance of the J-33 engine at high humidity and pressure altitude above 85 degrees. John told me he wanted the "old-T" right on the end of the runway, so I went slightly right before turning left to line up for takeoff. "I said on the END of the runway— I've got it!" He stomped right brake, shoved the power up to 85% and taxied out into the grass overrun before turning back to the runway heading with the tailpipe hanging over the end of the runway. Then he said, "Now we're ready to go." So, we went to full power and released the brakes. Then he told me not to force it off—let it fly itself off—so I eased the nose gear off at 85 knots and noticed the trees on the end of the runway were getting awfully close. We broke ground and I called, "Gear up." By now we were past the end of the runway and climbing so I called "Flaps up." "No, no!" he exclaimed from the back seat. As we started out over the bay, he said, "Okay, flaps up." I hit the paddle switch forward. He said, "Now look behind you." When I looked back I saw the trees coming up to our altitude as we sank over the bay with the flaps up. It was a good thing John had flown out of Keesler before and knew about hot weather takeoffs on that short runway.

Since I was flying from the front seat and John wasn't exactly forthcoming about his night out with the three women he had been with, I wasn't too surprised when I didn't hear anything from the back seat and even found that the instrument hood was in place back there. So I was on a solo cross-country back to Reese AFB. No sweat, I made sure he was back with the living before we landed and that was the name of that tune.

Next came a max-range dual cross country that we would do in one day—out and back. We started out at 0700 with 813 gallons of fuel and set out for McDill AFB in Tampa Fla. The performance charts showed that we could make it that far if we step-climbed to 40,000 ft and we were right on the edge of the range chart even with an en route descent at 89% power. Once we arrived in the high altitude structure we started to increase our altitude a couple of thousand feet every 15 minutes or so as we burned off fuel.

At about 37,000', with aileron boost off due to the thin air, we negotiated the last 3000' very gingerly with the canopy frosting over, heat on max, no other traffic to worry about out over the Gulf of Mexico, straight to McDill. About 120 miles out, we started our descent at about 300'/minute and with the fuel gauge barely above the E mark, landed straight in on that 400' wide runway that looked much shorter than it was. After a rather bad landing due to the odd landing picture on such a wide runway that was made for B-47 formation take offs, we just had enough fuel to taxi into the transient ramp and shut down just before flameout. The good ol' performance charts hadn't lied even though we'd almost gone off the edge of them.

We took our time on the return trip and made a refueling stop along the way at Columbus AFB Mississippi, another ATC Training base, not a base that was training in the T-37 like Spence AFB in Florida. I never regretted having to train in the T-34 and T-28 instead of the T-37. One peculiarity of the 6000# "Dog Whistle", outside of its piercing scream of its twin J-85 jet engines, was its propensity to spin upside down, a very hard maneuver from which to recover. One instructor and student never did recover and spun in. The Flight Manual boldly declared that if recovery wasn't complete by 10,000', ejection was the only alternative. The spin recovery in the T-33 was fairly easy, stick forward to break the stall, rudder full opposite to the spin direction and recover with the nose slightly below the horizon. I never wanted to try any spin recovery in a T-37. I had another cartoon in the class book that showed a slicked back Instructor from Bainbridge AFB with a T-37 under his arm, NO STEP written across the wings and the

Instructor saying," I just brought a li'l ol' T-37 up from Bainbridge to show y'all."

The only problems I ever had in the T-33 were awe inspiring and completely unforgettable. The first was the only time John ever yelled at me—the "No! Don't raise the flaps!" was mild by comparison to the time we were making an instrument approach to Lubbock Intl. and when it was time to put the flaps to ¼, prior to intercepting the glide slope for an Instrument Landing System (ILS), I looked down at the approach plate to check the intercept altitude. As I did, the airspeed was decreasing near the stall. Noticing that I had put the flaps full down, I said I was going back to ¼ where they belonged. Without any power increase, we were just about "parked" at 2500' and too little airspeed when John yelled, "I've got it!" and shoved the power to max, dropped the nose and gave it back to me to continue our instrument approach. After the missed approach, he merely exclaimed, "Don't ever do that to me again!"

The second time was during my formation final check ride. We had to go from four-ship trail formation to four-ship echelon. As I came to join on #3 in a right banking turn, all three T-33s ahead of me rolled out with me as #4 in a 30° degree bank closing in—oops! I had to cut power, roll wings level and fall in as #4 on the wing—all in about 2 seconds. When I rolled out in perfect position, having put my right tip tank up, over and back from the tip tank of number three, my check pilot found his voice to say, "If you hadn't pulled that one out, I'd have "pinked" you and sent you home." All I could think of, was if I hadn't pulled that off, we'd have been splattered all over Loveland Texas.

The T-33 was such a joy to fly, I could have taught my wife to fly it—without having to lie at dice about it—but the most fun of all was "cloud chasing". Between 10,000' and 25,000' flying between the cumulous buildups in west Texas was like a game of hide-and-seek. You could fly right at a big towering cloud and just at the last minute, zoom around it, between two or three of them and try not to get caught having to penetrate a line of them. That could be dangerous—adding a bit of a thrill to one's solo flight.

One day I was manning the RSU (Runway Supervisory Unit) out between the landing runways with my clipboard for grading student landings for the class behind us and my binoculars (the better to check your landings, gear down and flaps, my dear) when I noticed that there was a rather large "cumulo-bumpus" to the west of the field. As I watched it climb up the window panes in my little glass cubicle, I called the weather shop and asked if they were tracking this building storm on the CPS 9 Radar. They said it was already at 45,000' and growing, plus it was heading our way. When we halted all local flying and secured the RSU with all the T-33s on the ground, the top of the storm had passed the last pane of glass in the RSU. I was told to evacuate and truck back to shelter. The top of the storm had hit 56,000' and it was hailing in Leveland, about 8 miles away. You wouldn't want to be "cloud chasing" with one of those.

Another one of John Gardner's quotes was: "If I say EJECT and you say WHAT, you're talking to yourself."

With the end of Basic Pilot Training, came the much

anticipated Assignment Selection announcements. Since I was 18th out of 24 at the end of training, I wasn't surprised that all the fighter assignments were already taken—the F-100, F-102 and F-104, even the F-86 in Johannesburg South Africa. That was already promised to our Luftwaffe student, Ernst Seivers, for whom my wife had stayed up most of the night before graduation sewing his insignia and GAF wings on his uniform. The only assignments left were C-124, KC-97 and one WB-50 in Sacramento California. John said, "I don't know what a B-50 is, but I advise you to take it."

CHAPTER 4

ON OUR OWN - FIRST ASSIGNMENT

New Blood

It was a great decision to follow John's advice. I found out that the B-50 was a first line bomber in SAC, which replaced the B-29 until it was replaced by the B-36, B-47 and eventually the B-52. I knew something about the B-29—the one that dropped so many bombs on Japan, eventually ending WW II with the B-29, Enola Gay, dropping the Atomic Bomb on Hiroshima. It had bigger engines and a higher tail, R-4360 engines instead of R-3350 that powered the B-29. It was an awesome air-machine to a shiny new 2nd Lt. on his first assignment right out of pilot training. First, there was a brief stopover at Stead AFB outside of Reno Nevada for Aircrew Survival Training. This was a humbling experience for a brand new crewmember. The program included parachute training, from a tower platform, not an airplane, being dumped out of your pilot's seat head first into a swimming pool in November with helmet, flight suit and boots and having to surface, swim to a 20-man life raft and help others to do the same.

WB-50 Near McClellan AFB, 1962. Bigger than a B-29, fun to fly, but hard to land. I was actually in the left seat when this was taken.

One of the most arduous portions of the program was the 5-day trek through the beautiful California/Nevada border countryside. After 2 or 3 days in static camp learning how to build a fire, make a shelter, purify water, keep matches dry, make manzanilla tea, using a compass and all the good-to-know things that all survivors need to have experienced in preparation for the real thing, we were ready for the 5-day movement exercise. After sitting around camp for three days, we were broken down into 9-man crews, given an onion, a potato and a live rabbit and told to follow our local area map to the rendezvous point some 15 or 20 miles away through the forested, hilly countryside that was half in Nevada and half in California. So, off we go into the wild green yonder with our meager rations, back pack with shelter half, ground cloth, canteen and compass. Each of us had a chance to navigate for a time and we were progressing well along the route. The first hour was a pleasant stroll through the forest on pine straw and a temperature just above freezing. As the day wore on, it started to snow and it became colder. Since we were trudging into the wind, all the guys in front showed their green fatigue backs, but as the snowfall increased and we had our first rest break, everyone could see that, although green in the back, we were all white in the front. By the end of the day, the snow was about a foot deep and it was time to stop walking and build a shelter for survival. It was also time for all nine of us to share our meager rations—our bounty consisting of the rabbit and some stew vegetables. The guardian of our cuddly, furry white meat source had become quite attached to his charge and was not about to do it in so we could all share it. But then nobody else wanted to do the deed either. So, it was left up to one of the instructors to do it for us. He showed us how, with the quick flip of the wrist, to make our now limp rabbit ready for skinning. This could have been a problem except that one of our enlisted crew members was an avid deer hunter and knew how to skin our tiny "dear". After all the fur is removed from a rabbit, as Flip Wilson would say, "That don't leave much rabbit." Cut into 9 pieces, each of us had a less than a sumptuous entrée to go with our onion, carrot and potato in boiled water and washed down with our manzanilla tea.

Due to the cold temperatures at night, we had to keep our water bottles from freezing, so we kept them close to our bodies in the sleeping bags. We also had to keep our cigarettes and matches dry. I managed to rollover on my water bottle, displacing the stopper, so the contents ran down inside my fatigue pants into the side pocket where my cigarettes and matches were located. Needless to say, I had a soggy mess to dry out while we were still in static camp before our trek had even started.

One of the most basic things we learned while in static camp was how to start a fire. One piece of survival equipment, in addition to the machete, a very essential piece of survival gear, was a small piece of flint. The machete was instrumental in shaving chunks of wood to make tinder; grass, leaves and pine needles also became basic fire-starting materials. On sunny days, one could use a magnifying glass to start a fire, but since none was provided in our survival kit, we had to learn the "flint and steel" method. Every crewmember was required to demonstrate his skill at achieving enough sparks to ignite a small pile of tinder before adding twigs and branches for a roaring fire.

One drawback we found toward the end of the exercise was while sitting around a warming camp fire, especially inside a tent or other enclosed space, outside of not burning it down with too big a fire, we were burning pine wood and the smoke therefrom caused all of our noses to turn black breathing in the soot from the fire. We all had blackened handkerchiefs before we went home.

While on the 5-day movement exercise, we had to deal with a foot of snow a day for four days. After the third day, we were having a bit of a problem plodding through the ever-increasing snow. The answer to our dilemma of not being able to move much farther than we were at the time was snow shoes. Not many of us had ever been on snow shoes before and after a little instruction on their usage, it fell to me to lead off as a trail breaker in knee high snow. With very little nourishment and no previous experience on snow shoes, I soon reached the point where I couldn't put one foot in front of the other. Our intrepid Airman First Class Instructor approached me and said, "What's the matter, Lieutenant, having a little trouble moving ahead?" I had to admit that I would rather somebody else break trail for a while and I would help keep us on track with my trusty map and compass. Then it became an endurance race to keep up.

However, at the end of this ordeal was our chance to practice our shelter-building abilities. I had kind of hooked up with Ron Hurst, with whom I had gone through

T-28 training, and since we were both going to McClellan AFB together, we became a two-man team to build an overnight shelter. Ron was a deer hunter and outdoorsman, so with his tutelage, we found a huge downed tree which became the foundation of our "fortress" in the snow. We cut 4 or 5 lean-to poles to form an A-frame upon which we draped both our shelter halves, piled beaucoup pine boughs on top and left only a small entrance port with four sticks just inside stuck in the ground upon which we could mount our boots upside down to dry. All we had inside our snow cave was our sleeping bags, a candle, two chocolate bars and two cigars. After two or three hours inside, we were drying out and the temperature was up to almost 50 degrees. When the sun came up in the morning, the snow had covered over our shelter and we could hear someone calling us to come out and join the rest of the miserable crew, but we were so warm and dry we didn't want to burrow out and face another day of slogging through 4 feet of snow—until the leader called, "If you don't come out, we'll tear your shelter down!" That did it, and out we came. By this time, we were looking a little grungy with dirty noses, pile caps with ear flaps down, and four days growth of beard. The picture of us taken that day made me look like "Pierre, ze great French Trappeur".

By now, we only had one more night on the trek and then an escape and evasion exercise back to the original camp site. The night had to be spent out in the open with less snow, but no shelter, just our double sleeping bags and ground cloth. Ron and I ended up in our sleeping bags at 0 degrees temperature, under the North Star with our half chocolate bar eaten and just half a cigar sticking out of our sleeping bags zipped up to our chins.

After recovering from that night, we had to try to make it back to the compound without being caught and thrown into prison camp. This required each of us to escape-and-evade, E&E, through the arid and cold Nevada countryside and reach the finish line before the school cadre could intercept us and take our ID tags. Two comical events occurred before we were all captured and thrown into "Stalag- 17".

The first was my attempt to blend into the sage brush as a camouflage technique that had been taught in E&E class. As I was making love to that clump of sage brush, two Instructors approached my position in the darkness and one said to the other, "That looks like sage brush." If I hadn't giggled at their facetious comment, I might have gotten away with my subterfuge—or not! But they shined their flashlight on me with their hand out and I had to surrender and head off to prison camp.

The most bizarre occurrence was ones' student's attempt to outrun the opposition to cross the goal line before he was apprehended. Since the end was in sight just about 50 yards ahead, he took off at a dead run in the dark toward the lights that represented freedom. Unfortunately, he couldn't discern the 3-strand barbed wire fence that was actually the internment camp perimeter. One second, he was running full-tilt in one direction, the next second he was rebounding in the opposite direction having caromed off the wire and was found on his backside with three red stripes across his shins, waist and chest. He was the only one who wasn't laughing.

Having been starved and exhausted in the frigid wilds of Nevada, it was time for the final phase of survival in the early days of the Cold War by following the lessons acquired during the Korean War.

During a classroom demonstration in Air Force ROTC at Washington University, we listened to a tape recording of an interrogation by a Major Mayer of a POW who had recently been repatriated by the North Korean Communists back to the United States and from whom the Army hoped to learn more about Russian developed "Brainwashing". This was the buzz word de jour in 1954 post Korean War military parlance. The interviewer asked this POW why one of his comrade-in-arms had perished in the harsh winter weather outside the hut in which they were interned. "Why was he outside the POW quarters?" "Well, he was thrown out because he had Dysentery and he was smelling up the hut." "Didn't you think it would hurt him to throw him out in the snow?" "We had to think of all the others and we decided he couldn't stay inside and possibly infect the rest of us." This was a very graphic example of what we, as future Air Force Officers may have to face if ever captured. Now it was time to find out for sure if we would be up to rigors of being held captive by the Communists.

The most humbling experiences of the course was being interrogated at all hours of the day or night by big, nasty, billy-club-toting enemy guards to whom you had been drilled from day one to give only name, rank and serial number. When that didn't satisfy your captors, you were instructed to tell false stories about what your mission was, where you came from and who your commanding officer was—all things that supposedly would lead to a more lenient treatment, but never did, because they already knew, or said they did, all that information. I'm just glad I didn't have to experience the real POW treatment. That was realistic enough for me.

By the time we were told we were through with Survival Training and we could proceed to our first duty assignment, we were not only hungry and dirty, most of us were broke from trying to learn to gamble at more than Liar's Dice. I had found a nice quiet kind of Mom and Pop motel and bar where the owners were so pleasant and friendly, that I hadn't realized that their little bar games had cost me more than I could afford to lose. No wonder mom and pop were so easy to like—and it was not their first Survival Class of new students. The only good part of my Reno gambling introduction was having a classmate, Joe

Machaud, try to teach me how to shoot Craps. We played at one of the closest casinos and the only thing I remember about Craps is what the Stick Man said when Joe rolled an 8, "Eight, easy eight, three ways to make an eight—front line skinner, back line winner, Ace don't play and Craps don't pay!"

Before leaving all this fun and enlightenment behind, a couple of us headed to a local college hangout in order to replenish our lost calories and gain back the 8-10 pounds we'd lost. The "Deal of the Day" caught my eye on the sports-oriented menu—a Touchdown Burger with French Fries and a Chocolate Shake. Well, it certainly looked like it would fill the bill when it came and it did a bit more than that. I could only eat half of it and was so full I was about to blow up. However, by the time I had driven half a day toward my forthcoming assignment, I managed to finish it and save myself the price of another meal.

Now came the daunting task of reporting into my first duty station as a slick-wing, young 2nd Lt. who didn't even know what a WB-50 was, what the mission was, where we would be living and whether our household goods, meager though they be, would arrive in time or if at all, in general, where this Air Force career was going to take me and my bride.

When introduced to each of the seasoned veterans of the 55th Weather Reconnaissance Squadron during the first few days of in-processing, to a man they said, "Ah, new blood" as they pumped my hand. Still a young, 2nd Lt., I was "New Blood" as well.

After drawing all sorts of equipment from the 538 Section—Equipment Issue—I had flight suits in green and orange, flight jackets, summer and winter weights, an A-3 and a B-4 bag, boots, helmet, survival knife and on and on— everything a new WB-50 co-pilot would need for weather reconnaissance missions, mostly over water or snow. Little did I know whether I would need any of it, but glad to have it to load into my A-3 bag and stow it in the bomb bay for each mission.

So, here we go—checking out in this huge, 4-engine beauty—the B-50. As a new "Dumb-s--t co-pilot, I was subjected to many a seasoned Aircraft Commanders, Instructors and Check Pilots during my check-out phase of training.

One of the best was a senior Captain who was a whiz at instruction and instrument flying, especially in the simulator, but as I found out later, not too well thought of as a Mission Commander. I never found out why, but I did learn why he was so-well respected as an Instructor, especially on instruments. When two other co-pilot trainees and I were flying a training mission with Captain Waller, we were subjected to a series of instrument approaches in the right seat into Mc Clellan AFB, Beale AFB and Travis AFB, all within the local area for the WB-50. During the last hour of our training mission with the #2 co-pilot in the right seat, the weather had become so marginal that Approach Control required us to RTB—return to base— the visibility had become so bad that we might have to go to an alternate landing sight. Since I was in the observer's seat and had access to the radios, I was elected to re-file for an IFR (Instrument Flight Rules) clearance. While I was scouring the Enroute Supplement for the proper procedure to file an IFR clearance to a suitable alternate, I was informed by Capt. Waller that we were going to land at our home base and nowhere else! Having informed ATC of this fact, I and the other new co-pilot proceeded to learn a very valuable lesson about instrument approaches in lousy weather conditions. Somehow, we (he) managed to find the murky way to the end of the runway while we neophytes sat in the co-pilot and observer seats and looked at the approach plate, the Instrument panel the gauges and each other as the "Instrument Guru" explained how he knew exactly where we were every minute, even with half the instruments not working. He was able to make the runway lights appear suddenly in front of our bewildered eyes just as we descended to absolute minimums for a precision approach. At 100' and 1/4 mile visibility, the runway was in sight and we landed right on the numbers. The explanation of how we achieved this feat is too complicated and would only be meaningful to someone who knew about instrument approach procedures, about ILS, localizer, outer marker, holding patterns and VOR-DME. We were still not sure about all the particulars, but Capt. Waller was sent to Tinker AFB to be the head simulator instructor for all B-50 students from then on. I didn't get to go to TTU (Technical Training Unit) until four or five months later. Before that, I had another course to attend.

Shortly after arriving on-base and finding a suitable house less than a half a mile from the entry gate to Mc Clellan AFB, we were settling into our new home, which our "good friend" Don Wright had found for us at the very reasonable price of $11,900, we were informed that my first TDY (Temporary Duty) would be to Alaska for Arctic Survival School. I explained that I had just come from 4½ feet of snow during Aircrew Survival Training, but that didn't seem to matter to the Training Section. If I was going to be flying missions to Alaska periodically, I had to attend Arctic Survival School.

So now, my young bride, after a year or more of Pilot Training, was to be alone for two weeks while I enjoyed my first of many TDY's in our 2 ½ years in California.

If I had thought Nevada in December was anything like Alaska in February, my conception was abruptly changed as soon as we landed on the frozen runway at Eielson AFB, of course in the dark, since it was already 4PM, 13 ½ hours and four time zones away from California. There wasn't 4 plus feet of snow, barely 4 inches, but it was about

15 degrees below zero and even without a wind chill, it was a breath-taking introduction to Alaska in a 1961 winter. We had donned our winter gear for the 15 minutes or so it took us to load our personal bags out of the bomb bay and on to the crew bus. Then the ground crew towed the WB-50 into the cavernous Birchwood Hangar, built by the Russians in the 1930s. On subsequent missions in below zero weather, the crew would actually load up, go through the Before Starting Engines checklist inside the hangar with all the heaters operating before being pushed out through the 150' wide doors onto the cold, dark ramp to start engines as soon as cleared by the ground crew. Flying was usually suspended at 40 below because by the time the Co-Pilot and Flight Engineer started No. 3 and No. 4 engines and the Aircraft Commander and the Flight Engineer started No. 1, the oil in No. 2 had frozen and it wouldn't turn over.

The most memorable part of Arctic Survival School, outside of the cold, was the exercise where each crew had to prepare for a survival ration drop by helicopter sometime during the final two days. We had to have our rescue code panels of orange and white parachute cloth set out for the helicopter pilot to see where to drop and we also had to have our sleeping bag canvas outer covers filled with snow in order to douse our signal fire that was waiting for their arrival. Since it was so cold and the air was so still, our crew heard the raucous H-21 (with a T-28 engine in it) crank up on the ramp at Eielson some 18 to 20 miles away.

Therefore, we had the "drop" on the rest of the students, lit our pine bough fire and as soon as we heard the H-21 airborne, we dumped all our snow on our beautiful raging fire. It had taken hours for us to fill these bags because the humidity was only 3% and even filling a canteen cup with snow and trying to melt it for drinking water took pounds of snow just to yield a cup of water. Unknown to us, there was an inversion layer at about 1200' with below freezing air beneath and 40° degree air above the inversion layer. With our smoke signal billowing up like an A-bomb cloud, it hit the inversion layer and spread out in all directions causing a huge dense cloud layer over the entire valley to the extent that the helicopters pilot couldn't see the ground anymore. Since ours was the only signal they could see, they made only one drop, right next to our encampment. We received all 5 cases of C-rations. With plenty to eat and the weather warming up to 32 degrees above zero instead of the forecasted 30 degrees below zero, we had to trek out to the rendezvous point with unused cases of C-rations carrying most of our survival gear instead of wearing it while in shirt sleeves and the melting snow falling off the trees overhead.

Following my indoctrination to Alaska in the winter, I would have many have many more experiences in the 49th state both in winter and summer. The most startling difference is the temperature spread and the fact that one seldom sees the sun in the winter, while the sun seldom sets in mid-Summer. In the winter, walking to the O. Club or BX, is done on squeaky, frozen snow, rarely over an inch deep. If it is below -15 degrees, you had better have "fat-man" pants, Mukluks, a parka with a hood over your earmuffs and heavy mittens. If you're not appropriately dressed, the Air Police are authorized to pick you up and take you to a nice warm jail. One woman tried walking from the Housing Area to church in a skirt and boots. She received frostbite on both legs and was hospitalized.

The summertime brought its own unique hazards in the form of swarms of large mosquitos. Two descriptions of the Alaskan mosquito were "Big enough to stand flat-footed and f--- a turkey." The other describes a Crew Chief who put 5000 pounds of JP-4 in one before he found out it wasn't an airplane. I personally swatted one off the wall of the BOQ with a towel and it left a blood spot on the wall the size of a half-dollar. One day, three of us were walking to the BX and I had to tell my Navigator not to stop—there was a swarm of mosquitoes right behind his head. I never saw "Half-Slow" move that fast again.

Another summer hazard in Alaska had to do with fishing in the lake on base. After 4 or 5 hours, in an open boat, it became necessary to find "relief". If one were to find relief over the side of the boat into the lake, the mosquitos were poised to attack. Of course, the snide comments from your fishing mates didn't help the situation. It's hard to pee, laugh and fight off mosquitos all at the same time.

Flying in Alaska, especially to the North Pole and back, had its share of boredom as well as excitement. As the saying goes, flying is "hours and hours of boredom, punctuated by moments of stark terror". One of those moments befell a crew commanded by an RAF exchange officer during a Ptarmigan mission to the North Pole. During a lot of those hours and hours, the boredom was suddenly broken by a runaway propeller on number 1 engine. (Since I heard about this mission during one of ours also to the North Pole and it was over 50 years ago, I'll preface the rest as "hearsay") It seems that while trying to shut down the runaway propeller, part of the propeller broke off due to the cylindrical force and, missing the Number 2 engine, embedded itself in the Nav. Compartment which immediately depressurized the airplane and caused a great amount of wake turbulence from the now motionless Number 1 propeller and the portion sticking out of the left side of the airplane. Along with this condition was a lot of drag from the dead engine adding to the control problems already associated with the loss of an outboard engine. With the Number 2 engine now at almost maximum power, the crew returned to Eielson by the most direct route and was able to land without losing any more engines or propellers. I also heard that the RAF Exchange Officer won the Victoria Cross for that brave deed back in his own country.

The boredom started early in my co-pilot career, as the Aircraft Commander (A/C), with whom I flew most often, used to brief before take-off to Alaska: "I'll take it to lift-off, you take it to Eielson". As soon as we had the gear in the well, following the After Take-off and Climb Checklist, which included a cup of coffee from the Navigator to the A/C, he would put his seat back and feet up so he could rest a bit. I couldn't put my seat back, ever, because the Flight Engineer's station and panel was right behind me back to back. Now it was my airplane for the next 8 or 10 hours. That is why I called him: Gear-up, coffee-on Kesselring. Of course, he had a nickname for me as well; Young Fester— no idea where that came from, but it stuck. Once we were at cruise altitude, autopilot engaged, radio calls, fuel readings, course headings were complete, there wasn't much to do for the balance of the 13 ½ hours that most missions ran but listen to traffic, tune the radios until out of range over the Ocean, make sure the weather observations were going as planned every hour as well as the fuel log and power settings were adjusted, and then eat your flight lunch after the "point of no return" where it is shorter to proceed to destination than turn back to home if a serious emergency arises. This requires a bit of coordination with the Navigator and Flight Engineer. After his nap, the A/C would take over so the Co-pilot could stretch, move around, pee in the navigator's briefcase (right next to the relief tube), or take the required hour stint at the engineer's panel. This required repositioning the four Mixture Controls to Auto Rich-(Otto Rich, The German engineer) for 5 minutes then return to Manual Lean-(Manuel Lean, the Mexican Engineer) then resetting the RPM to the next lowest setting in the Performance Manual and reducing Manifold Pressure across the board to follow the curve for 99% of Max Range Cruise. Each Co-pilot was required to do this at least once every mission, Fortunately, Flight Engineers were not required to make any Co-pilot approaches or landings, even though they all thought they were more qualified than the Co-pilots.

One such Flight Engineer was barracked with us in Chachako Hall at Eielson when a rather large moose decided he'd rather be inside our quarters than outside in the lovely spring weather. It had managed to intrude into the hallway about 6 or 7 feet when one of our intrepid crewmembers discovered its presence between us and the exit door. Being not only an avid deer hunter as well as a gun enthusiast, our "just out of the shower" towel-clad Sergeant retreated to his room and still clad only in a bath towel, brought out his Great Western .44 Magnum six gun with which he intended to become the first moose-slayer on the crew, or anywhere else that we knew. Fortunately, our combined cooler heads prevailed through the logic of: "If you shot that moose in here, how are we ever going to get it out of here?" Logic prevailed over the hunter instinct and, with towels, calm voices, like one would use on a pet dog, we persuaded the moose to back out of the hallway after having punched several holes in the hallway plasterboard. It sure beat trying to drag 1500 pounds of dead moose outside—then what would we do with it?

Speaking of moose-hunting, our navigator was able to go with his father who owned a butcher shop in downtown Fairbanks. He shot a moose that was the 33rd largest one ever shot in the State of Alaska and the largest ever shot north of the Kenai Peninsula. After bagging this 1500 pound moose, he and his father dragged it by sled into Fairbanks and proceeded to butcher and package it. In 1961, the town of Fairbanks still had dirt streets and board sidewalks, a throwback to the Wild West, so it wasn't too hard to sled a 1500 pound moose on the frozen snow to the butcher shop and reduce the meat to chops, ribs and moose burger—no refrigeration required. With it all wrapped in butcher paper and appropriately labeled, we not only loaded the bomb bay with the meat, but also the 6 ½ foot moose rack that had a 30.06 slug crease in it.

By the time we arrived in California, the meat was still frozen and the rack unharmed. The weather was McClellan winter standard—WOXOF, which is weather 0, obscured, 0 visibility and fog. So, we had to practically bust minimums to get home. After skillfully negotiating an almost 0-0 landing, we were taxiing back up the parallel taxiway when "Gear up, Coffee on" stopped the airplane. He dropped the bomb bay doors forward and told the Radio Operator to climb out his hatch and come forward with a roll of copper radio wire. Meanwhile, he had the Navigator retrieve his coveted moose rack from the bomb bay and hand it up to me leaning out of the co-pilot's window where I was able to hand it up to the Radio Operator right above me. He then instructed him to wire the rack to the ILS antenna on top of the nose. This accomplished, we buttoned up the airplane and everyone returned to his station while we taxied in, still in near-zero visibility. As we approached our parking spot in the Squadron area, we had a junior Airman marshaling us with lighted wands. As he gave us our signals to turn, slow down and eventually stop and shut down engines, we noticed his eyes growing larger and larger as we reached our spot. At last he gave us our shutdown signal. As we deplaned, we could see him staring up at the moose antlers attached to the ILS antenna. Don then explained that the reason we were late was that the "Antler Deicing" went out on us on the way home.

On the days we weren't "visiting" the North Pole on our "Ptarmigan" weather recon missions, we occasionally had time to ride the bus into Fairbanks. In 1961, Fairbanks was nor much of a city. It was more like an 1880 wild-west town still with board sidewalks and few paved streets. The people who lived in and around there were like Pioneers and certainly had that spirit. One bar downtown had a sod roof over a log frame and catered to Bush Pilots. They pretty well owned the bar and sat around with their chairs tilted back, hats on the back of their heads and beer and whiskey bottles on the tables. You didn't mess with these guys.

There was one bar outside of town where the Air force bus stopped on its way into Fairbanks and on the way back to the base. One day, I was with some of my fellow crewmembers sitting around the piano bar with the buxom blond piano player/owner when Fred "the Navigator" said aloud during a pause in the conversation and music, "God, I wish I had a little pussy!" Immediately, our entertainer said in response, "So do I, Honey. Mine's that wide" with her hands about a foot apart.

One night, I decided, since I had missed the last bus back, that I was going to walk the rest of the way to Eielson AFB. I was going to walk home from the Buffalo Saloon at about Mile 16, only 10 to go to the base. As I was shuffling along the snowy roadside wondering if I would ever make it before I froze or was run over, a car stopped in the center of the icy road. Seeing my salvation right in front of me, I trotted to the passenger door, asked if he, and she, were "Going My Way". He was a Major stationed at Eielson and told me to hop in. After thanking him for saving me, I noticed two things. The first thing was the fact that the Major was "schnockered", evidenced by the fact that he was sliding from side to side of the frozen highway and was leaning over the steering wheel glued to the windshield. I sobered up enough to realize we were in danger of not reaching our destination in one piece. The other thing I noticed was sitting right next to me. She wasn't bad looking, even in heavy winter outerwear, almost unnecessary with the car heater blowing hot air at us, but rather exotic looking none the less. As I looked at her profile, I saw high cheekbones and somewhat almond eyes. So, I asked her name and introduced myself. She said her name was Jeanie Elia and she was from Tanana Alaska. I knew where Tanana was, but I still had to ask her about her nationality. My guess was Filipino, but she looked at me rather dumb-founded and said, "No, you dumb---t, I'm an Eskimo!" I would have liked to have seen her again, but she was on her way to Tanana and obviously more interested in the Major, her ride home, than me, about to be home and thankful for it.

One of the most demanding of our Air Weather Service missions was called the "Wagon Wheel" where an aircrew was dispatched to Hawaii for two or three missions, then on to Alaska for two or three more before returning to McClellan for a much needed R&R (Rest and Recuperation) for 8 days.

One of my earliest mentors in the 55th Weather Recon Squadron was a "seasoned" Major named Vic Whittier. He was, in addition to a senior Aircraft Commander and all-around good guy, also the Squadron Supply Officer. His office desk had a sign that read: "Supply—what if you don't have enough of, your war doesn't run as well as if..." He advised me on house party etiquette telling me to fix pitchers of Martinis and his favorite, Manhattans, so the guests will lay off the good stuff. Well, I looked up the recipe for both, had the pitchers brimming with olives and cherries for garnish and only had two takers for our promotion party. Everybody else wanted our bourbon, scotch and vodka for their drinks. I also found out that First Lieutenant promotion parties last a very short time, attesting to the kindheartedness of a great many senior and well-meaning squadron mates for their "New Blood".

One of the aircraft with which we shared hangar space was the U-2 spy plane. It was fascinating to watch one take off and climb out of sight within the field boundary. When one would land, the ground crew would park its truck alongside the approach end of the runway before touchdown and a pilot would radio the landing U-2's altitude in feet over the end of the runway until a second before touchdown at about 25-30 miles per hour, when he would be advised: "6', 5', 4', 3', 2', 1—Touchdown!" The truck would run alongside until 2 crewmembers could hold the wingtips level before installing the "Training Wheels" under each wing so it could taxi back to our shared hangar.

One night, we were on a Ptarmigan Mission to the North Pole when a U-2 contacted Anchorage Center and requested cleared airspace from its present position to an emergency landing base in Texas. When the controller asked for airspeed, the U-2 pilot replied, "Classified." When the Controller asked for altitude, the U-2 pilot again replied, "Classified." Upon further query as to time enroute and altitude, all the controller was told, "Where I am, there IS nobody else." Following his flame-out, the U-2 was flight followed to a "dead-stick' landing in Texas.

During our first California summer in our little 1150 square foot, flat roof, striated, green and white first real home, Sue and I encountered our first Sacramento Summer. "How Hot Was It?" During June and July, we had over 30 days in a row where the temperature reached 100 degrees or more. One could count a dozen grass fires from the traffic pattern. By the end of June, we had to go to Roseville and buy a swamp cooler which we installed in our bathroom right across from our bedroom pointing right at our bed. In the evening we would walk down to the root beer stand and buy a quart of ice-cold root beer, sit on the back porch in our skivvies and try to stay cool. Even our Siamese cat, "Slasher McSnagnasty", would lie on the kitchen floor and pant. Then, the most violent weather we had in winter was moderate to violent fog. Palm trees instead of pine trees, but since our weather recon missions went to Hawaii and Alaska, we were used to hot and cold weather.

As mentioned before, the Wagon Wheel saw both extremes during the winter months. One such mission was not scheduled for Major Vic Whittier and his crew. Since they were prepared only for a "Loon Echo" mission to Hawaii and return, they hadn't packed cold weather gear for the Wagon Wheel. Once in Hawaii, they were informed that no aircraft or crew was available for the next "Ptarmigan" mission to Alaska. So after two missions in Hawaii, the crew headed to Alaska direct without any arctic gear. About half way there, number 3 engine started to run rough and Vic and the Flight Engineer decided to shut it down just past point of no return. After another hour or so, with land in sight, the Flight Engineer said he didn't think he could keep number 2 engine running much longer. Since they were due East of Kodiak Island NAS, they declared an emergency and headed directly for a straight-in landing. With both inboard engines inoperative there was no hydraulic pressure and two generators were off-line. Without brakes and only the outboard engines with which to maintain directional control, the crew was at least able to get the landing gear down and flaps to 30 degrees. After touchdown, the B-50 rolled and rolled right to the end of the Navy runway. After shutdown, the emergency over, the Aerodrome Officer pulled up in his staff car with the red light flashing and screeched to a halt right next to the nose gear. When the Flight Engineer opened the nose wheel hatch, half a roll of toilet paper came up and hit the deck up front. The Engineer asked, "What's that for?" "That's for you, we already used the other half." When the crew deplaned, the AO explained, "If you'd run off the end of the runway, we'd have just left you there and painted you gray." Sure enough, there was an R-4D about half a mile up the hill and it was painted gray. Maybe it served as an incentive for everyone to remain on the runway.

Now the aircrew was stranded on Kodiak Island until a double engine change could be accomplished. Since they had only packed for Hickam AFB, they had to appear in the NAS Officer's Club in aloha shirts while all the Navy Officers were in dress black uniforms.

WB-50 - The difference between the WWII/Korean War B-29 bomber is that these B-50's were modified with R-4360 engines, a larger rudder & two F-50 foils outboard of #1 and #4 engines for air sampling as well as a "shoebox" E-1 with filters that could be changed hourly from the rear fuselage compartment. It induced a considerable amount of (flat-plate) drag which made it difficult to climb to 30,000 ft. for high-altitude sampling. (I'm in the left seat in the window above the "A" in AIR)

Now it was our turn to attend TTU, Technical Training Unit, at Tinker AFB in Oklahoma City. This was the school for new aircrew members to learn all the many technicalities of the B-50 (WB-50, KB-50, RB-50, plus the KC-97 and C-124 aircraft.) Sue and I packed up and drove our Studebaker Silver Hawk all the way down to Oklahoma and took up residence in a second floor apartment in Midwest City right across from Tinker AFB. Three memorable occurrences befell us in our six weeks in the land of Okies who park in the front yard and watch for tornadoes.

The first event happened to Sue driving my precious Silver Hawk to the grocery store. In Oklahoma you have to expect some wind, be it a breeze or a tornado, but in between there are occasional gusts to 40 or 50 knots, and so my sweet wife of only a year and a half opened the car door and it was blown out of her hand and folded against the front fender. This rendered it almost unusable for future use. Therefore, we traded it in for an American Motors Rambler, a red convertible with a black top—a 3500 pound 2-door with a railroad car frame to give it strength and stability.

The second memorable occurrence was in Midwest City and was called a tornado warning. As 7PM approached on a Sunday evening, we were in our 2nd floor apartment after dinner watching the Ed Sullivan Show when the normal wind dropped to zero, the sky turned green and the TV issued a tornado alert for the area. I immediately went down to the Texaco station on the corner and asked if I could put my brand new red convertible in his garage. Of course, the owner said if we had a tornado there wouldn't be any safety in his garage, so we just waited and watched as the greenish hue faded into nightfall and the warnings disappeared. We found out on the 10 o'clock news that a tornado had touched down about 8-10 miles Northeast of Midwest City and had done considerable damage.

As for the third memorable event, I had checked out in the Tinker AFB Aero Club T-34. I had learned that college friend and fraternity brother—also a Washington University ROTC graduate—was now undergoing Basic Pilot Training at Webb AFB in Big Springs Texas, just 2 or so hours down the road from Tinker AFB. Having notified Ike of our Saturday arrival, we proceeded to Webb AFB and after a couple of hours reminiscing about college with Sue and Ike, catching up on old times, I strapped my bride in the back seat with instructions to stay off the intercom and radio. After Ike saw us off at the ramp, I decided to show him what a hot pilot I was, so, after takeoff I held the T-34 just off the runway until the landing gear hit the well and I had 120 knots airspeed. Then I pulled the nose up to about 30 degrees and started an aileron roll to the left. Unfortunately, I had not considered the fact that FAA required civilian (Aero Club) T-34s to modify the controls with bungee cords to put the "feel" in the maneuvers rather than control by position. Fortunately, I had enough airspeed and altitude to complete the roll with my feet on the stick to keep the nose from falling through the upside-down portion of the roll and the wing tip only cleared the runway by about 3 feet. After completing the roll and thinking how impressed everyone on the ground would have been, Sue found the intercom button on the rear throttle and exclaimed, "Don't you ever do that again with me in the airplane!" To aggravate her even more, I got kind of lost on the way back to Tinker. For the second time, Sue found the intercom button and this time said, "We're lost, aren't we?" Fortune prevailed again due to the fact that I was low enough to regard a passing water tower with big letters GUTHRIE on it. "I know exactly where we are, we're in Guthrie Oklahoma and only about 30 miles from home."

At TTU the aircraft simulators all had loud, blaring sirens that announced to everyone anywhere near that someone had just crashed the simulator. Since I had a particularly sadistic simulator instructor, I managed to cause that siren to go off rather frequently. His favorite trick was to have the flaps split on takeoff. I should have a "heads up" by the scanners in the back if we were a "real" airplane, but since the "unreal" airplane didn't have scanners, so about the time the simulated landing gear left the simulated runway, the simulated airplane would roll to the inverted position and the siren would announce that "Dumbshit" had just crashed upside down.

Following several weeks of training in Oklahoma, we returned to California in our shiny new Rambler convertible. When we went to register our cute red ragtop, we were informed that we would have to pay a 4% use tax since it had been purchased in another state. Since Ronald Reagan had become Governor of California and was kicking 1000 welfare recipients off the state dole every day, I gladly paid the California Use Tax, even though we couldn't afford it.

Now we came to the everyday Air Weather Service routine of Alaska one week, home for a week or R&R and training, then off to Hawaii for 8 days.

Besides the contrast in the weather between the two destinations, Eielson AFB in Alaska and Hickam AFB in Hawaii, the time differential was the same. We gained 4 hours enroute to both, but arriving in sunny, warm Hawaii, somehow the bag-drag and trip to the housing office was only a minor inconvenience on the way to a night of "fun and frolic", hopefully, between the "Wahini Kapu", the Officer's Club outside bar, and somewhere in downtown Honolulu. But first, one had to go to the Officer's Club Cashier and cash a Kelly Field National Bank counter check for $20 or $25, and be sure you called home to tell Sue to deduct it from the checking account. The call was placed through the PACAF Command Post via MARS (Military Air Route Radio Service). Then off to town in our 1948 Cadillac, after putting 2 or 3 dollars worth of fuel in it—never saw the tank over 1/4 full—but a Dollar went a lot farther in 1960 -1963.

The first destination of course was Fort DeRussy on the beach at Waikiki, a very valuable piece of real estate owned by the US Army as an R&R haven but much coveted by the hungry land developers in Hawaii. With $25 or so in one's pocket, it was time for a couple of beers at the rustic

Fort DeRussy bar, a stroll on Waikiki Beach before dark when all the "Beach Bunnies" were getting ready to go out on the town, then maybe, a trip over to Chuck's Steak House for the best steak and salad in the whole area. Located about two blocks off the beach in a rustic old house, the salad was served on the mantle buffet style while the menu was painted on Lancer's wine bottles in white letters. The only thing to order was how you wanted your steak cooked and how big a one you wanted, or could afford. People lined up around the block to get in by 7PM.

Honolulu, in the early 60s was more of a military town than the glitzy tourist destination it has become and after the Vietnam buildup, it became even more so. One of the seamier quarters was called Hotel Street, the hangout for a lot of sailors as well as some local inhabitants. One night I took the Cadillac down to Hotel Street and went into one of the many bars. Having found a young "lovely" sitting on a bar stool, I asked for a dance. When she stood up, she was about 6 or 8 inches taller than I was with tight white Capri pants, long dark hair and a sexy blue blouse. I asked, "How tall are you?" "I'm 6 foot 5 and a half, Bob" she said in a deep voice. On my way to the "escape hatch" I had to pay for my beer. The bartender said, "The only two women in this place are me and the owner over there at the end of the bar."

Then, once in a while, we'd go to the Royal Hawaiian and have a $5.50 Mai Tai—only $3.00 at the Wahini Kapu.

We'd sit there and call ourselves "easy money" The only other attraction that we would have time to enjoy was driving around to the Pearl City Tavern and partaking of its marvelous Chinese noodle soup and listening to the large parrot talk dirty from his cage. Evidently, the Sailors at Pearl Harbor taught him well.

More about the Wahini Kapu. This was located right next to the two-story swimming pool and snack bar. Wahini Kapu is Hawaiian for women not allowed, supposedly a stag bar. I spent more time there than I should have, but that is where I met Janice—definitely a wahini—also the wife of a Navy Lieutenant who didn't know that his "worse half" was looking for fun with the Air Force rather than across the inlet to Pearl Harbor. Unbeknownst to me, she had been seeing a KB-50 pilot, so when she appeared one night when I was there, I found her very friendly and started a rather brief but enjoyable romance with Janice. Since she was not unknown to B-50 pilots, we developed a system of announcing our arrival in hopes of inviting our friend to jump on the ferry and be sitting there when we arrived. We would open the nose wheel hatch and throw all of our flight lunch boxes and assorted garbage into the hole. As we approached the Outer Marker for the ILS approach into Honolulu International, we would pass over Ewa Beach where Janice and her husband lived. Just as the needle swung, we would have the Flight Engineer hit the Nose Wheel Down switch and all the trash from 700 or 800 feet would fall into her yard, so she would know we were only 45 minutes away.

However, one such evening, I was there at the bar when the Navy Lieutenant entered instead of Janice. The first person of interest to him was the KB-50 pilot that had been the first of Janice's friends. The Lieutenant went up to "Doc" Muffley and exclaimed, "I'm looking for a young Air Force Lieutenant who's been playing around with my wife!" Well, Doc retorted, "I'm a Major, not a Lieutenant and it's been a long time since I was young!" Fortunately, he didn't know I was the one he was looking for, even though he had been the first to start the "Janice Watch" a year or so before.

One night, without finding Janice at the Wahini Kapu, I was going to put my idle time to good use by writing a letter to my Mother. For about an hour, I drank 2 or 3 Cuba Libres, with 151-Proof Rum, while trying to update dear old Mom on the heroic exploits of the Weather Recon world. Evidently, the more I drank, the more loose and downhill my writing became until I finally realized that not only what I was trying to write was becoming both incomprehensible and illegible, but I had exceeded the limits of the paper and was scribbling on the green felt table top at which I was sitting. It's a good thing someone pointed that out to me and dragged me back to the BOQ before I mailed that sloppy letter. I still remember that "monstrous" curb that I had to navigate outside the Club bar.

Our aircrews each had a trusty old car at Hickam in which to cruise the beaches. In our case (pilots) we had a dark green '48 Cadillac. The Navigators had a black '48 Buick and the weathermen had a Studebaker of roughly the same vintage. The salty air in Hawaii had done a number on the Studebaker, so the Weathermen decided to repaint it—kind of a mossy green, with buckets and mops. We called it "The Mop-job Special". It was no beauty, but it got them where they wanted to go. One of those was the golf course at Lilahui. Whenever a Weatherman named Mike would play and forget to wear his hat, his bald head would turn bright red and we'd tell him, "Hey, Mike, Your Grimes light is stuck." (Grimes Light is the rotating beacon on top of the B-50).

Hawaii wasn't all fun and frolic. We did fly weather reconnaissance missions every two or three days per crew. We flew both day and night, high and low altitude out over the Pacific Ocean for 13 ½ hours at a time. One of those missions required a climb to 300 milibars, or 30,000 feet. Even going out at 10,000 '(800 mb), or 18,000' (500 mb), when the time came to climb to 30,000' we put on all the Climb Power we could produce, but the last 2000' almost required a "sky hook" and a winch to stagger up to FL300. Then, after burning down fuel to less than 9000 lbs, we had to descend from our lofty perch to cross Kuhuku Radio Beacon below 10,000'. With the RPM restriction of just 1800 Rpm and 20" of Manifold Pressure, we would flutter down until we could extend our arrival path way south of Honolulu so we could cross Barbers Point beacon at pattern altitude for landing at Hickam AFB.

One of these letdowns took us out over the path of an outbound Aircraft Carrier heading away from Pearl Harbor. The Aircraft Commander decided to have a little fun with the Navy, so we set up a landing pattern with Mixture Rich, RPM 2350, Gear Down—Before Landing Checklist, and flaps 30 degrees. At about 200' on final approach, the LSO was giving us a frantic wave-off, noting that our wing span was longer than the flight deck was wide, and, besides, our tail hook wasn't down. We had fun anyway looking at all the uproar on deck as we made our missed approach and roared off to Hickam.

While the 55th WRS was flying missions out of Hickam, we were tasked to provide weather recon for the US Army's launch of a missile up to 100,000 feet with an Atom Bomb on top and detonating it in the upper atmosphere. Well, the Agena Rocket wasn't as reliable as the Army thought it should be, so we were able to enjoy the hospitality of the Fijian people for 2 or 3 days.

On the way to Nandi (now Nadi, but still pronounced Nandi), we had to cross both the Equator and the International Dateline. Upon arrival at Nadi International Airport, and securing suitable maintenance facilities, and fuel, we were left on the ramp with our wingtip hanging over the chain-link fence, but were informed that it would be secure in that location. Before we left, we saw lots of local kids with bicycles grouped by the fence staring at the strange airplane with United States Air Force on the side. We were delivered to the Macombo Hotel, a rustic hostel built and operated by two retired PANAM Captains. With a palm frond "Burri" over the front entrance, an open lobby and a cozy bar, it was an ideal haven for our "World weary" crew. The first "refreshment" we found in the lobby was a Mississippi River brown liquid in a wooden fountain that was a local product called Kava. It wasn't alcoholic; it was a narcotic, unbeknownst to us foreigners, and it was ground from the root of the Kava Tree. After a cocoanut shell-full of Kava, we repaired to the lounge for a few Fiji Lagers, the local alcoholic brew. After a few of each, we were joined by a C121 crew which also had a reconnaissance role in the upcoming great event of the launch of the Agena Rocket with an A-Bomb on top. After a night of "soaking up the local culture" and sending the harried bartender to his just repose, we finally called it a night and retired to our rooms. After an innumerable number of hours therein, it was time to find something to eat, so I found my way to the hotel eating establishment, or snack bar. After ordering a snack, but nothing from the bar, I noticed that the sun was close to the horizon and streaming in through the window. Having crossed the Equator as well as the International Dateline the day before, I didn't know if the sun was rising in the East, or setting in the West, I noticed one of our

Scanner/Radio Operators sitting at an adjacent table. Since my watch showed 5:30, I asked the Airman, "What time is it, Bush?" As his smile broadened, he replied, "5:30, Sir." After a suitable pause for effect, I asked, "All right, Smartass, AM or PM?" After almost falling to the floor with laughter, he replied, "PM, Sir, the sun is going down. I knew you didn't know what day it was—Sir."

Since the Army was having a bit of a problem with its Agena Rocket, and therefore the launch of the A-Bomb into Space, we had a lot of free time, during which I had the opportunity to do some sightseeing around Fiji. One of the most pleasant sights in Nandi was the beautiful wife of the very proper and stodgy Immigration Officer who had officiated during our arrival on the Island. With his very proper English accent, official uniform complete with cloth billed cap and green tabs on his knee socks, with shorts and tunic plus swagger stick, I could only assume that this very "un-proper" wife would enjoy the diversion of showing me around the local area. As it turned out, we embarked on a day-long sight-seeing tour of the cocoanut plantations by rail from Lautoka to Sigatoka and return with a stop or two for the opposite of Rest and Relaxation—I know I didn't want to rest and she never encouraged relaxation.

After the Army finally decided to release our Weather Recon detachment for return to Hickam AFB, Russ Kilmer decided to make a departure that the local Fijians would remember. Since most of the locals wore skirts, shirts and sandals, or bare feet that looked like frying pans with 5 handles, we thought our daytime departure would rouse them from their Kava-induced rest under the Banyan trees. Before take-off, we requested a left turn out of traffic which was approved. The turn took us around to the location of the Mocombo Hotel, and with climb power set, gear down and flaps 30 degrees to keep the speed down and the noise-level up, the effect on the hotel was to blow off the rattan "buri" over the entrance and probably the wrath of the owners plus some sleeping Fijians under the Banyan trees.

We had returned to Hickam pursuant to going back to McClellan when the Army finally managed to launch the Agena rocket with the A-bomb atop up to 100 miles in the atmosphere. I was sitting outside at the Wahini Kapu swimming pool when the detonation occurred about 9:00 PM. I saw the sky light up in the West, and for 15 minutes or so, you could read a newspaper by the yellow, green and blue light on the western horizon. Years later, I saw a picture of that sky in a coffee-table book by TIME/LIFE almost 45 years later.

The second extended deployment for my young career came in 1962. At a pre-deployment party at the Officer's Club on 25 Feb 1962, we were informed that we would be the Weather Recon portion of a large task force during an operation out of Christmas Island, 1050 nm south of Honolulu, Hawaii. Designated Task Force 8, and commanded by a Brigadier General, we became officially known as 8.4.2.1. The entire affair was called Operation Dominic and we were going to be responsible for tracking and reporting the weather conditions for several A-bomb tests near Christmas Island. We would have a major input for the success of the tests.

While enroute to our Island Paradise, the Aircraft Commander addressed the entire crew over the intercom, telling them that after our tour of unknown duration, we would be eligible for R&R in either London or Paris. He started a list around to the rear of the airplane so each enlisted crewmember could indicate his choice of either London or Paris. While the "boys in the back" were making their decision, I had the foresight to look at a local area chart of our destination and noticed that Christmas Island looked a bit like a pork chop with a lagoon in the meaty part with the runway and base area on the bone part. I also noticed that there were two villages on either side of the lagoon. They were little more than a collection of shacks that we found out after a couple of days were where the locals lived who worked on the base. They were called "Konyos" and surprise! The two villages were named "London" and "Paris".

Once established on the U.S. side of the Christmas Island complex, we settled into the routine of mission briefing, flying a day, trying to find something to do on a nearly deserted island and eating in the Holmes and Narver contractor's tent, which was tasteful and fattening—lots of meals, lots of calories, but very satisfying, from steak and eggs at 0430 before a mission, to roast beef, mashed potatoes and gravy for dinner—we ate well! When it came to drinking, we were restricted to water, iced tea and "bug juice" (Kool-Aid). We also had "Mission Whiskey". Mission Whiskey was a fifth of "Good ol' Gukenheimer's" which nobody could stand. We had a myriad of fruit juices available through the Contractor's Dispensary, but the only juice that would cut the taste of "Good ol' Gukenheimer's was grapefruit juice. Regardless of what one tried to cut it with, the mission whiskey would eat through the bottom of a paper cup and take the handles off in two drinks. The officers tried to foist it off to the enlisted crew members, but they couldn't stomach it either.

One of the most prized commodities on the Island, outside of fresh water, was one ice machine. Similar to what you can find in any motel corridor now, and during the heat of the day, it was usually pretty well emptied by the end of the day by crewmembers trying to cool off the "Good ol' Gukenheimer's" and fruit juice. But before any mission, we would raid the ice box and fill up our jugs for the B-50 to be consumed only with water. That was another commodity that was rather precious due to the fact that the best way to fill the water jugs was to wait for a rather frequent rain storm, wait until the rain on the barrack's roof washed off the salt and sand and then place the jugs under the corrugated eaves and collect fresh rainwater—mighty refreshing during a 13 ½ hour mission.

After flying our first mission out of Christmas Island, we were scheduled for our first look, in attendance, for an A-Bomb detonation. We were all lined up on the ramp before sunrise with our goggles on, facing away from the blast area about 25 miles away, when the countdown over the loud speakers went to zero. The first thing we noticed was a brilliant flash of light, too bright to look at, even with the smoked goggles on. I peeked under the dark lenses and everything I saw was as bright as noon and it was only 0530. The next thing that came our way was the booming echo, then, right behind that, came the pressure wave from the blast. We were able to stand by that time and watch the red, yellow, purple and gray cloud climbing up to 20,000-30,000 feet. Out of the corner of my eye, I saw the palm trees bending, the tails of the WB-50s flapping, and then the shock wave hit us standing on the ramp in awe. It felt like someone had just punched me in the chest with a boxing glove. About 15 seconds later, all the trees and tail planes shook again as the secondary shock wave raced through and took all the air out of our lungs from the negative pressure.

One of our missions involved flying at 18,000 feet within 25 miles of Ground Zero. When the countdown reached zero, we were ready with our goggles on and our sensors on. Within 2 or 3 seconds, the sky lit up as bright as the sun, even in the morning daylight. Then we saw the colorful signature "mushroom cloud" which went from red to blue to purple to pink in the growing sunlight. At this time, the Aircraft Commander said, "Okay, boys and girls. Get your Brownies out and take a picture of this!" As we were looking out the windows and observation blisters at the towering cloud, the first shock wave came through. With the Autopilot engaged with barometric altitude control on, and in a 20 degree bank around Ground Zero, the shock wave buffeted the B-50 to the extent that the half empty fuel in the wings sounded like oil cans: "Kerplunk, Kerplunk!" It felt like the wings were going to come off— then the secondary wave came through and the airplane seemed to float sideways, finally rolling straight and level with both of us on the controls. We had punched off the Autopilot and were back in control. I said, "I'll bet you never do that again!" We made a point of briefing the other crews on that point.

APPROX 25 KILOTON BLAST (BEFORE SUNRISE)

STAND BY FOR SHOCKWAVE(S)

CHRISTMAS ISLAND 1962

A-BOMB BLAST - Waiting for the blast wave to arrive and the unbelievably bright light to fade. About 15 seconds after this picture was taken, all the palm trees were bent over towards us and the B-50 tails fluttered in the wave of high pressure. When the negative pressure came back through, the reverse happened and it sucked all the breath out of us. WHAT AN EXPERIENCE!

We flew one more mission before the "big bomb" was detonated during the test series. It was supposed to be a 650 kiloton device, but a slight miscalculation wound up a 1.3 megaton shocker. When we returned to the Island, we heard that the chow hall tent down on "A" Site had been incinerated. Our barracks had roof panels caved in, but the jalousies were still intact since they were always open. Inside, I noticed that my metal bed was in the middle of the floor and my shoes and Monkey pod carving of a Tiki God were all the way across the room. I was glad we had been in the air and not on the ground for that one.

During our stay with our British hosts, we had two memorable conversations with the very proper Controllers. The Departure Control for Christmas Island had been established as 333.3 UHF. As we lined up on the runway for takeoff, the Tower Controller would direct us to "Contact Departure Control on a "handful of threes".

The second conversation was as equally one-sided, "I say, 'Calcimine', use caution on the taxiway, there's a bit of a bump out there." Well, that bit of a bump turned out to be a 3" drop into and out of a sunken asphalted-over steam line across the parallel taxiway. Our 189,000 pound airplane fell into the drop-off and out again, nearly knocking off my headset and nearly hitting my chin on the yoke. All I could reply was, "A Bit of a Bump?"

I did manage to leave a memento on Christmas Island in the form of B-50 tire marks. One of my first missions in the left seat was coming to a 13 ½ hour end. After lining up with the runway over the lagoon, I had called for "Manifold 22"—22 inches of Manifold Pressure— "RPM 2350, Gear Down, Before Landing Checklist." Instead of adding a couple of inches of Manifold Pressure (Throttle) myself so we could make it past the end of the runway, I continued stretching the glide until the airspeed was down to the stall speed. Just as the water ended and the concrete started, we touched down without even a bounce since the airplane was through flying and slid to the concrete with a sigh instead of a squeak—not as loud as the sigh I let out when I finally exhaled. I barely needed to brake as we rolled slowly toward the first turnoff. I guess I had adopted a motto of: 'He who adds power on final shall be known as a 'Phynque'." A couple of nights later, we were taxiing out to the runway end for takeoff when the Flight Engineer turned around in his seat and pointed to the heavy black marks on the very end of the runway illuminated by the landing lights. He said, 'That's where the Goddamned Copilot landed the other day!"

One of our missions besides routine weather reconnaissance was atmospheric sampling of radiation from non-US A-Bomb testing. One particular sampling project followed the Russian 50 Megaton blast in Siberia, the fall out cloud from which the radiation was drifting, made it all the way from Alaska, through Canada and across the Atlantic Ocean where it contaminated an Aer Lingus DC-8 which had landed at Shannon Ireland. The airplane, passengers and crew were quarantined.

With satellite weather imagery and the International Space Station, the Aurora Borealis can be seen on TV news and National geographic channels. But in 1961 or 2, I had heard of the Northern Lights but the first time I was more or less alone up front and began to see the blue, green and white waves or ribbons of glowing ice crystals I was in awe. I called the A/C and Navigator up to look and they were kind of blasé about such a display. "Oh, we see this all the time in the winter. Haven't you ever seen it before?" I was almost speechless. It looked like I could add power and climb right up to the "waterfall", but I was assured that it was impossible. What a sight, especially for a 24 year old new co-pilot!

During one of our missions, we were carrying an Airman Technician in the back with the Dropsonde Operator who had a sampling machine that directly measured the intensity of the radiation that we were collecting during successive orbits up in Central Canada. After an hour or so in a left-hand orbit, constantly checking the prop hubs and wings for icing in our own contrails, the Airman said he was really picking up good readings on his "Whizbang" sampling machine and asked if we could remain in this orbit for another hour or so. The AC asked, "How hot are we getting?" The answer from the back was "We're up to Scale 6, Sir." The next question was, "How high does it go?" The scary answer was, "Scale 6, Sir." Then he added, "If you haven't eaten your Flight Lunch yet, I strongly advise you to do it now." After a second request for more time in orbit, the Weatherman in the nose, the ranking member of the crew, stood up, turned around and exclaimed, "Bullshit, we're going home!"

Since I had flown the T-34 in Primary Pilot Training at Malden and one was available at Eielson in the Aero Club,

I decided to take a summertime jaunt in the local area. I had met a nice school teacher, at least I thought she was nice, who taught at the on-base school and was seen occasionally at the Officer's Club. After we shared a couple of *Champales* together, I had the brilliant idea that I could really impress her by taking her up in the T-34 for a little "joy ride". After takeoff, I showed her around the countryside where we had chased a couple of moose up into the Brooks Range with our WB-50 and were still up there. As we headed back towards Eielson, I decided to make a low-level pass down the Cheena River. We were at about 30 or 40 feet over the tortuous river, dodging overhanging trees and rocky outcrops, when I called the tower for landing. They asked me for my position, since they couldn't see me. In order to enter the traffic pattern on a downwind leg, I pushed the power up and at about 130 knots, zoomed up to 1200 feet in a second or two. My passenger found, not the intercom, but the tower radio and exclaimed, "I think I just wet my pants!" I was sure the tower controller had a good snicker at that as did I. I found out that she was less than sweet and innocent when I went to visit her downtown in Fairbanks. She had a top floor apartment in the Northward Building, a rather luxurious high-rise that I know I couldn't have afforded for any length of time. When I went up to her door and knocked, I heard some muffled sounds of scurrying and mumbling. When she came to the door, she had on a robe and told me to come back later. Now it dawned on me what she was doing between school terms to make a living). As I was leaving the Northward Building, I had a beer or two in the first floor bar. I decided to try to find a way home at midnight and opened the door to the parking lot. As I did, the sun hit me right in the eye. I closed the door and returned to the bar, saying, "I think I'll wait 'til the sun goes down." The bartender told me I was too late—that the sun had already gone behind the hill and was now coming back up! It was still better than having it dark all the time and having to wear a parka and Mukliks.

After one of our eight-day trips to Alaska, all the way home I kept thinking about pizza and pitchers. It was winter in Sacramento, but the weather was still fall-like, about 57 degrees, no wind with fog and no wind. I jumped in my black, sporty Austin Healy with the top down and headed for Shakey's Pizza Parlor.

Shakey's was an old fashioned, downtown watering hole, that not only had pizza, beer and free peanuts in the shell, thrown on the floor when through, it also had a jazz band. I would order a pitcher of beer, a Supreme pizza with anchovies and listen to the Capital City Jazz Band. These guys played all kinds of music, but the tune I remember the most was "Does Your Mother Know You're Out, Cecilia?" Words can't describe the picture of the almost bald bass player who sang the refrain in his undershirt with the final word—"Ceceeeelia?" After half a pitcher of Bud, pizza and the goofy look on his face, big ears sticking out under his floppy hat, I used to fall on the floor laughing.

In 1962 we were in the midst of the cold war with Russia and its desire to place ballistic missiles in Cuba. In the event the Cuban missile crisis was going to escalate into an invasion or bombing, the Air Weather Service was called upon to provide reconnaissance (weather?) around Cuba.

The trip to Kindly AFB Bermuda was really smooth. We requested direct routing at 25,000 feet, a really good altitude for the WB-50. We were below the FL300 commercial airliner altitudes and above the mostly prop-driven executive traffic. With a nice tail wind, we cruised directly east through the ADIZ (Air Defense Identification Zone) right on our estimate. Bermuda was clear and a million so approach and landing on the British maintained island was smooth and easy.

Bermuda is really pleasant during nice weather and we expected some smooth missions. The day after we arrived we were able to rent motor bikes, the main form of transportation around there, and go sightseeing in and around Hamilton and the beaches. As we were coming around the end of the runway on a tour of the surrounding area, we saw one of our WB-50s running up engines before takeoff. One of the locals on a motor bike didn't take notice of this and blissfully rode right behind the running aircraft. He was riding straight and level one second and ass-over-tea kettle the next. The prop wash blew him right in the ditch alongside the road. He never saw it coming—it was hysterical!

Since the local weather was so nice, we expected some smooth missions. The day after our arrival we were able to rent motor bikes and go sightseeing around Hamilton and the beaches. We even had time to hit the Class VI Store and purchase some inexpensive beer, wine and whiskey for transport back home. One of the most popular wines, (Vin-de-jour), was *Rose Mateus*, a light, somewhat effervescent pale red wine from Portugal which was in great supply at Kindly AFB. My navigator and I stocked up with a whole case of it and stashed it behind the BOQ counter where the clerk could keep his eye on it.

During our next day off, the weather had turned to nearly hurricane proportions with winds up to 50 knots and horizontal rain. The housing units on Base had garages underneath and some of them had rainwater up to the doorsills of their cars and washers and dryers afloat. Since the O. Club was shut down, Bill and I decided to go downstairs and sample at least one of our stash of Portugese wine. After the first one, we decided it was so good we might as well have another, then a third. That did it. We saved the rest to take home.

Finally, it was time for our crew to take its turn flying recon around Cuba. The mission took off into the sunset and headed south for a 10 hour night recon for about 50 miles around the Island. About half way up the northbound track, the weather turned really nasty with thunderstorms across our path. While the Aircraft Commander was back in the nav compartment making sure we were well out of Cuban territorial airspace, I was all alone in the right seat when we ran smack into a big "thunder-bumper" and I had to disengage the autopilot so I could hand-fly the pitching, bucking aircraft. Actually, it was flying me and I had to call for help, just as the A/C jumped in and buckled into the left seat. I couldn't tell whether I was right side up or upside down at that point. Fortunately, Russ took over and kept us more or less level until we passed through the turbulence. During radio contact with the preceding mission crew, we were told that it was pretty smooth for their mission. -HA!

Since the reason for our trip to Bermuda had been resolved, we packed all our goodies and plotted our return to McClellan. Since The A/C was busy accumulating some last minute "goodies", the job of flight planning fell to me and Bill. I even filed the clearance and was ready to board when the rest of the crew arrived for the trip home. About half way across the country, the A/C asked out of curiosity how long it would be for total time enroute. I told him, "Ten hours and 50 minutes." He was somewhat skeptical of our calculations until we were in contact with Sacramento Approach Control. It looked like we were going to land exactly 10 hours and 50 minutes after take-off. From the back of the airplane on interphone, one of our enlisted crewmen remarked, "I guess it's easy to be on time when you have the throttles in your hand."

One of my favorite places to eat while stationed at

McClellan AFB was a charming roadside bistro in Vacaville California called the Nut Tree. The menu was very eclectic with a great variety of soups, salads and sandwiches served in an open-air dining area with great views of the surrounding mountains and countryside. The décor was very modern with lots of colors and fabrics—just a delightful place to be even with the usually crowded conditions. It was a pretty easy drive from San Francisco, so it was a well-known gathering spot for Yuppies and Preppies.

Also located at Vacaville, adjacent to the Nut Tree, was a small airport, the most endearing feature of which was a glider school. Well, the first time I saw those graceful, soaring gliding machines being towed into the air with such ease, I had to get in on the fun of powerless flight. I signed up for my first instructional ride, paid the $35 for a navigator trainer pilot to tow me in his sweet, hot little Super Cub to 3500 feet, and after some much needed explanation of air currents, stall speeds, cable release and handling capabilities, we were off. The glider was sleek, cream-colored, light weight and had only two wheels in the center. The tow cable was attached to the nose and after it played out behind the Super Cub, it became taut and we started moving down the runway. The wings leveled immediately and in about 5 seconds, we were off the runway. The instructor held our altitude just above the tow plane's tail with the cable arcing up to our nose. He demonstrated correct and incorrect positions behind the Cub, sliding out to the side to cause the cable to tighten as well as how to keep the cable taut when it slackens by cross-controlling allowing the slack to disappear. It was almost like formation flying, jinking back and forth and not letting the glider drag the tow plane from side to side or into a stall. Without any power of your own, you are at the mercy of the 150 HP in front of you, and you'd better "straighten-up and fly right" before you pull the cable release and are on your own. Now all you have to do is try to find updrafts and stay airborne until you run out of altitude and have to glide back to an easy grass landing. I returned two more times but was never able to solo. It is really a different way of flying.

In the Air Weather Service we had not just the WB-50s, we also owned two other types of aircraft, both jets, and both "Ramp Queens" (in constant need of maintenance and/or parts).

The "sexiest" one was a WB-47, a six-engine modified bomber in shiny silver and white with day-glo swooshes on the tail and engine pods. It was a real beauty, but unsuitable for everyday missions like we flew to Alaska and Hawaii. It had been procured from SAC, modified with screening foils for high altitude sampling of atom or hydrogen bomb clouds. One of my fellow co-pilots was chosen to fly this beauty but never enjoyed that upgrade because the WB-47 never fulfilled that mission.

The other high altitude bomber was a WB-57, a twin engine medium bomber called the *Camberra*. Its only pilot was Earl Stringham and one day he was scheduled for a post-maintenance test hop and I jumped at the chance to go with him for an hour and a half checkout. I signed out a G-suit helmet and mask and strapped into the back seat.

The visibility is great in the C-model with the long bubble canopy slightly forward of the wings. It is built close to the ground with big engines embedded in the wide, high lift wings which are started with a black-powder cartridge. We taxied out for take-off, briefed emergency procedures, and started our take-off roll. Those big engines were really loud and powerful and in 12-15 minutes of max climb, we were at 45,000 feet. After completing the required checklist items, I was allowed to play around with the smooth flying bomber until it was time to descend for approach and landing. Earl requested a "penetration", or rapid descent and was cleared to 10,000 feet, to report leaving each 5,000 feet. He pulled the throttles to IDLE, deployed the huge speed brakes and down we went. I watched the Altimeter unwind, called 35,000, then 30,000, 25,000, each about 9-10 seconds apart. At the 20,000 call, Approach Control said it was having trouble following us. We started our level-off about 14,000 feet so we wouldn't go through 10,000. The speed brakes came in and we leveled off so we could start our approach back to McClellan AFB. When we landed, the nose kept dropping until, from the back seat, I could see the runway ahead and thought the nose gear was not down. I was relieved when it too touched down and we taxied in.

CHAPTER 5

OFF TO MY SECOND CAREER

Jungle Jim, Here I Come

After three years of numerous 13 ½ hour missions to Hawaii, Alaska, Bermuda and Fiji, some of us were not going to continue in the WB-50, even though I had upgraded to Aircraft Commander with about 1400 hours in the airplane. This was the end of the WB-50 era and the finale for me also in the 55th Weather Recon Squadron.

Since the Vietnam situation was coming to action and the Air Commandos were looking for young warriors, I volunteered for the "Jungle Jim" Program. My orders came through for the 319th Air Commando Squadron at Eglin Auxiliary Field #9, which I found out later was Hurlburt Field,

Florida. There I found some guys who were dedicated to Counter Insurgency, or COIN.

Since I was going to leave "sunny" California with nothing of our first home after the 1962 divorce from Sue, all that remained to do was try and sell the house at 5620 Layton Dr. Since she left only that and took almost all the furniture, the cat, which she had ruined by having him neutered, and the car, for which I had substituted a '55 Austin Healy, I immediately contacted our "good friend" who had promised us that we would certainly recoup our $11,900 price we had paid for our little 2 bedroom "love nest" in 1960. Alas, he was nowhere to be found. A number of other people, I learned, were also looking for our "trusted" real estate agent, who shall remain unnamed in case others are still looking for him after 50 years. Since the divorce, I had had a couple of housemates, one of which was my former college and ROTC/fraternity buddy who I had so "impressed" at Webb AFB by doing the aileron roll on takeoff in the T-34. His first assignment upon graduation from Pilot Training was also at Mc Clellan AFB, flying RC-121s across the field. He and another copilot needed a place to stay that was close to the Base and inexpensive, so I rented the second bedroom to them for a little while until they found a bigger-and- better place. Since they flew long missions on separate days, they were seldom there at the same time, so the arrangement worked pretty well, except collecting the rent from the other 2nd Lt.

Since I now had an empty house, I looked for another housemate. When I saw a notice on the bulletin board at the Laundromat next to our favorite root beer stand, I called the number on the card of a female looking for a roommate. I talked her into coming to the house to see about a roommate for me, but she said, "But I am looking for a 'gearl'," in her French accent. When she arrived, I noticed immediately that she was not bad looking at all. As we were "negotiating" an arrangement, she said, "But I am not going to bed with you," as I backed her up against the heater panel with a kiss. Well, the living arrangement didn't work out, but I made her take her words back.

Since I couldn't sell the house, I did the next best thing. I rented it to a really sweet girl who had two children and was leaving her husband. The rental was a good deal for both of us and so I left California with her occupying the house and me being an absentee landlord—something I would regret later. So, I took off for Seattle, St. Louis and eventually, Ft. Walton Beach in my re-built Austin Healy.

About that beautiful, fun little car. It was black with red leather seats and top. The only problem I ever had was when I heard a bang and the 4-banger engine didn't want to run anymore. Evidently, it had swallowed a valve and almost needed the whole engine replaced. Fortunately, across the street lived a C-121 Flight Engineer who was skilled in engine maintenance and agreed to rebuild it for me. As he worked on that engine, he told me, "The deeper I go, the more trouble I find." I ended up having to replace the rod bearings, valve guides and valve stems as well as the broken valve and piston. But it got me from Sacramento to Ft. Walton Beach without any further problems.

That was some trip! Since the World Exposition was in Seattle that year, I decided to detour north and visit that corner of the country. The only memorable part of that trip was finding out that I had a floating astigmatism when I tried to see what time it was by looking at a large clock tower and was able to see about half of the clock face. It lasted about 20-30 minutes and was very unnerving. I could just imagine trying to read instruments or land at an unfamiliar airfield with only half of it visible. Slowly my field of vision improved until it was back to normal and I have only experienced it infrequently since. It is still bothersome, but I know it's only temporary and it has never returned while I was airborne.

From Seattle, I drove through Montana, the Dakotas, Iowa, and eventually to St. Louis. One incident occurred transiting the Black Hills before I came to the Badlands. I was slowed down on the downhill portion of the road, hardly a highway, because there was an older model car in front of me that I couldn't pass due to the many curves in the road. As I was maneuvering to get ahead of these four guys, an empty bottle (of Tequila, I think) came arcing in my direction so I had to swerve to avoid being hit by it. After 10 minutes of trying to find a way around those "Caballeros", I was finally able to pass them with my little rebuilt 4-banger at max RPM thanks to the agility of the Austin Healey, but as I went by, here comes another empty tequila bottle. I was glad to finally reach level ground, even if it was through the Badlands.

Upon arrival in St. Louis, I had a great reunion with my parents who had moved from the suburbs after I went into the Air Force, and now lived in the Greystone Apartments in midtown St. Louis. Near Gaslight Square, which Time Magazine called "The Great White Way of the Middle West." If one opened the window on the 6th floor, it was possible to hear the music and shouts from 2 blocks away. Some of that noise was Ragtime coming from the Natchez Queen, a riverboat replica where my brother-in-law played banjo and sang with the St. Louis Ragtimers— the only group on Gaslight Square that will not play "When the Saints Go Marching In"—since that was Dixieland and not Ragtime. On my last night at the apartment, Dad suddenly remembered that Cassius Clay was fighting Sonny Liston for the Heavyweight Championship. As I came out of the bathroom, he turned on the radio and we were just in time to hear the first round knockout by soon-to-be Muhammed Ali. What a disappointment.

CHAPTER 6

HURLBURT/FIELD 9

The Flintstone Air Force

The first person I met upon arrival at the 319th was the Scheduling Officer, whose motto was: "To err is human, but when the eraser goes before the pencil point, something is wrong!" He also wore my favorite squadron patch—"Have Goon-Will Travel".

So now it was time to learn to fly another airplane. Since I had flown three previous prop-driven airplanes, I had little trouble adapting to the "Mixture, Prop, Throttle" routine for adding or reducing power. In fact, I really took to the C-47, "Gooney Bird", even though I soon learned why it had acquired that nickname. On the ground, it was sometimes "awkward", but in the air, it was a graceful flyer. A cartoon in my scrapbook shows a young pilot being pushed toward an old bi-plane with an old hangar in the background labeled "Hurlburt Field". The old airplane had COIN on the tail and the young pilot is protesting, "But you can't send a young kid like me up in an old crate like that!"

The C-47 was the oldest aircraft in the Jungle Jim inventory, but was in good company with my old T-28, a couple of C-46s from the China, India, Burma Theater in WW II, B-26s from the mid-40s and 50s during the Korean War. Add a couple of C-123s- (It would be a nice-looking airplane if you took it out of the box it came in), some U-10s and you had the "Flintstone Air Force". Since I liked every airplane I had flown more than the last one I flew, I anticipated liking the Gooney Bird even more than the others. The history and capabilities of the C-47 were legendary from WW II and the Airline Industry as the DC-3, the first of which was flown about the time I was born.

One of its many exploits was documented in *FLYING* Magazine in a short article: DC-3

"At a point in the vicinity of Sutton, West Virginia, at about 0750E, a severe updraft was encountered which brought the nose up to the vertical position in spite of full forward pressure on the yoke. The plane continued on over until it was on its back, at which time the yoke was pulled to the full backward position to recover. For the next 20 seconds, normal flight was maintained at 3000 feet, but again a severe updraft was encountered and a loop was again made, recovering at 3000 feet. Following this, the aircraft was rolled over on its back and a half-loop was made, then it was thrown on its left side and at 1500 feet MSL the ground was sighted about 200 feet below the aircraft. Some altitude was gained but another loop occurred and the aircraft broke out of the overcast in a vertical dive with an airspeed of around 240 MPH. It required strenuous effort on the part of the crew to avoid striking the ground. Following this, conditions were again normal and the flight continued to Charleston and landed."

After many local training missions and before I could up-grade to Co-pilot, I was sent on a training exercise called "Water Moccasin" at Fort Stewart, Georgia with a crusty old (by my standards) Major who taught me many things about airplanes, counter-insurgency, women and cigars. The flying was mostly at night for both infiltrating "guerillas", supplying and re-supplying counter-insurgency forces para-dropping food and ammunition to those forces (both sides- we were easy) and acting as "umpires" during the late phases of the exercise. The actual coordination and the results of all this fictional war were of no consequence to me since we were players on both sides, but the experience of simulating actual counter-insurgency operations was exhilarating, plus the extra-curricular activities were equally enlightening. One such incident involved the Major's girlfriend—the "Chief Operator at Fort Stewart GA" -(which sounded like: "A'm the Cheef Oprata at Fot Stewart, yu'all"). Since this was fifty years ago, there wasn't much at

Ft. Stewart and she looked pretty good out there in the "Boonies". The only town near it was Ludiwici, and the "Chief Operator" was a 40 year old bleached blond who may or may not have lived up to her title. All I know is one night she and I ended up out in the back woods somewhere out the confines of Ft. Stewart with a bottle of vodka and a jug of orange juice parked in an Air Force blue Ford station wagon after observing an air drop in a large cotton field as part of the exercise. During our feeble attempt to turn around and return to civilization, I managed to land the Ford Station wagon in a roadside ditch with no way of driving it out to the dirt road we had taken to get there. So there I was, in a ditch, with the Major's girlfriend, just about out of vodka and orange juice about 1030 or 1100 PM in the dark, unpopulated backwoods of Georgia. After a couple of kisses and a little "petting", the only option left was for me to try to walk up the road and find some help to extricate the station wagon and the drunken blond from the ditch. As I came to the first bridge over the next ditch, I heard a very ominous hissing noise which I was sure was not a good sound to someone lost on a dark lonesome road, so I thought we were already in "deep serious", why not go back, be safer in the vehicle and wait for sunrise and possibly get lucky. Well, by daylight, I hadn't gotten lucky, but shortly thereafter, I did get lucky—a farmer with a tractor came down the road, and happily pulled us out of the ditch so we could find our way home.

Another memorable exercise found me as a co-pilot at a civilian airfield in Greenwood South Carolina as part of a Psychological Warfare element—a pre-cursor of much of my future endeavors as a C-47 operator.

One night, after our Blue Force Commander had "interrogated" a suspected terrorist in the corner of a tent with no clothes on, he found the suspect to be only a hardware store owner in downtown Greenwood, and definitely not part of the exercise. Some local firebrands decided to get even for the social gaffe perpetrated by our Commander. Even after furnishing the offended hardware store owner a hotel room and steak dinner at the local Holiday Inn, the towns people decided that, military exercise or not, they were going to show us a thing or two by doing physical damage to some of our "Flintstone Air Force" airplanes at "their" airfield. George Lattin and I received a phone call telling us about the "raid" and giving us a message to broadcast over our loud speakers to the invading horde. After copying the message, we hurried by cab out to the airfield and while George filed the local clearance, I got the C-47 ready to go. By the time I had number 2 engine started, George pounded up the cargo floor, strapped into the left seat as I started number 1, and we taxied out for take-off. After arriving overhead at 1500 feet, we cranked up the loud speakers and began our broadcast: "We understand you have been directed to attack Greenwood Airfield. This is neither sanctioned nor condoned by the Exercise Director. You will be held liable for any damage done to any Air Force aircraft." Evidently, our warning words were heard and heeded because no damage occurred—our mission was a success.

The next night we were assigned a "retribution" mission, which involved flying our loudspeaker aircraft over the Headquarters of the Red Team and turning on our alarm bell, normally used just for emergency bailout, with our microphone held up to it. At 3:30 in the morning, our reconnaissance mission became a "harassment" mission. As we circled overhead, we looked down as a T-28 was scrambling to come up and intercept us. We could see the pilot, whom we both knew, running the checklist, starting the engine, taxiing out and coming off the runway in his "Maytag Messerschmidt" to intercept us. At about 2000 feet, the "interceptor" made its first pass, as in shoot us down, but George called: "Gear Down" and chopped the power. As the T-28 whisked by, we raised the gear, applied full power and followed our "bandit" around a half circle with our landing lights on his tail. After a few more passes at us, "Tiger" gave up and went home to land back at his home base, while we returned to Greenwood and shut it down. When we were notified that we had been shot down, we protested that <u>we</u> had been the aggressor and should have credit for a "kill". Following the futile argument that we didn't have guns with which to shoot down a T-28, our Flight Engineer pointed out to the doubting umpires that, not only did we have a .30 caliber machine gun in the latrine, but that he had been a turret gunner on a B-17 during WW II. Good try, but no claim for us.

For my first check ride, for Co-pilot Qualification, the check pilot was a friendly guy with a good sense of humor. After I had checked out everything I could think of that a Co-pilot should be checking, I asked if I should sign the local clearance we were filing out of Base Ops. "No, you don't sign it, I'll sign it, because I is the F---or, you are the f---ee."

While training at Hurlburt, the Air Commando way was to start each day in fatigues and combat boots on the flight line with exercises before a mile or so run. Leading the pack of our young warriors was our late 40-ish Lt. Col Squadron Commander who was a distance runner of such prowess that he had trained to be in the 1954 Olympics—my junior year in high School. The one time I tried to outrun him, having been a miler and half-miler in high school and college, he took off like a scalded dog and was sitting in his office smoking a cigar when I finally and breathlessly reached the front door of the squadron. I never did outrun him.

Most of our exercises involved infiltration, exfiltration, supply and resupply of both friendly forces as well as guerillas. Shortly after the Greenwood exercise, I was ordered to Vietnam. In fact, I had to be replaced by another co-pilot so I could return to Hurlburt and pack up for an overseas deployment.

CHAPTER 7

VIETNAM

Here I Come

I only had time to pack my newly-painted foot locker with my name, rank and serial number along with the motto: "Have Goon—Will Travel". The next thing I knew, I was on a fully loaded MATS C-135 roaring down Hurlburt's runway, hoping it would get airborne before it came to the sand. Fortunately, it had B-Model engines and made it out over the Gulf. After a couple of stops in Hawaii and Guam, we touched down at beautiful Bien Hoa AB in Vietnam.

When we arrived at Bien Hoa, our new home for about 6 months or so, while we were unloading our baggage from the C-135, we were met by some outgoing personnel on their way back home. One of them was a B-26 pilot nicknamed "Dennis the Menace", who was being sent home by his commander a bit early in his tour. We found out later that he had been a bit overzealous in his pursuit of some "Charlies" in a sampan hiding under some trees along a river bank. With his eight .50 caliber machine guns in the nose of his B-26, this pilot went down to tree top level and blasted the sampan to matchsticks and the bad guys to pulp. However, all that fire power also chewed up the river bank throwing a shower of mud up into the right engine oil cooler, stopping it up completely, resulting in the shutdown of the engine, and an immediate RTB (return to base). After landing, the left engine was running so hot that it almost quit too. When I last saw Dennis, he was rather smilingly tipsy, wearing a pointed coolie hat and first lieutenant bars pointing down like a nurse's. When he took off his uniform shirt, he showed his T-shirt which had an American flag drawn on the back with the words: "I am a US Military Advisor, you cannot shoot me!"

There we were billeted in 4-man "Hooches" with a cot and a locker for furnishings. We had a refrigerator and a ceiling fan —otherwise, it was like camping out. The first 23 days in August it rained 20 days, causing one's bed to feel like a soggy mattress and if you didn't have your shoes and suitcase in the locker with a 75-watt bulb in it, the shoes and leather items would mildew and grow to the floor.

We started flying missions right away, only on our In-country Checkout, we spent a lot of time looking for a downed B-26 pilot and crew that had been lost up in II

Corps. The weather was always bad and the countryside was always mountainous, but we kept looking during our Special Forces supply missions without a sighting. After we had flown missions from I Corps, Da Nang, all the way down to IV Corps, Can Tho in the south, we had some really routine supply missions plus some really hairy ones. Whether it was an air drop or air land and off-load, the terrain, weather, unprepared runways and occasional ground fire were always concerns and continually tested our skills.

During this tour in Vietnam, I saw many new and exotic places from the air as well as the ground while we were resupplying the Special Forces. While down in the Delta, we would make a little side trip all the way down to Vung Tau, a coastal resort on the South China Sea, not a particularly scenic area because the beaches were dark sand and the water was kind of muddy due to the outflow of the Mekong River. However, there were usually some French bathing beauties laying out in the tropical sun, some with the top down, but who usually covered up upon hearing our spy-in-the-sky eye approaching for a low photo pass. My little pocket camera, <u>Minolta</u> never did get any good shots at Vung Tau.

I did, however, capture some shots out the windscreen of a couple of isolated landing strips like Dak Pek, Tuy Hoa West, Pleiku, Ban Me Thut and Dak Tho. We were scheduled to go into Dak Tho during daylight because it was almost impossible to find at night. It was right on the "Parrot's Beak", an outcropping of the Cambodian border and was a French rubber plantation which had come under the control of the Viet Cong, and alternately, the Khmer Rouge in opposition to ARVN and US Army, mainly, Special Forces. It was also one of the "off-ramps" of the Ho Chi Minh Trail into the Delta, or IV Corps. When we arrived, there was no welcoming party, only 2 or3 S.F. types and the beautiful wife of the French plantation owner, but instead of my desire to see more of her, we were told that after the M-14s were unloaded for the local forces, we were to take back a bunch of old Springfield '03s and "Didi Mao"—get out fast before the bad guys knew we were there. Our stay was therefore rather brief and we left with due haste for the relative safety of our home base, Bien Hoa. On the way back, I asked an Army Sargent what was going to happen to these obviously surplus Springfield '03 rifles and he said he was going to "appropriate" one for himself and that I should also. "Hell, Cap'n, nobody's ever going to use them, so you might as well take one home with you." Somehow, after careful disassembly of the action and barrel, I managed to get the useful parts back to the US in my foot locker and I still have the weapon—now with a new walnut stock from Bishop's in Warsaw Mo that I had checkered in Marianna Fla. It weighs about as much as an M-1 Garand, but it's a good hunting rifle.

Another "garden spot" to which we were directed

was a small strip up in the Highlands that didn't even have a name as far as I know. Some Army "puke" told us where it was and that we needed to land there for some reason—"not to reason why"—so we set up for landing on a really short field which turned out to be 1150 feet of downhill wet grass. Now, under ideal conditions, the C-47 can handle 1200 feet short field landings. As soon as we touched down, and Kirkpatrick called for flaps up, we knew we weren't going to stop in time, so he stomped on the right brake and ran the left engine to 30". The old Gooney bird swapped ends in about 50 feet and came to a stop just before the drop-off at the end of the strip with about 5 feet of the left wing tip in the pliable trees on the side of the "runway". In order to extricate us from the foliage, the Flight Engineer hopped out the over wing door and proceeded to use the aircraft crash axe to chop off the offending branches that were restraining our further progress back to the touchdown point. This seemed to infuriate the Province Chief for whom we had arrived since it was his trees that "Old Knothead" Willard Wyatt was chopping down. Somehow we managed to placate the Province Chief, or the Army-type with us did, and 20 minutes later we were back in the air, having demonstrated the Air Commando way of jerking a C-47 off the ground at 64 knots in less than 1100 feet.

Some of the questionable airstrips at which we landed were like muddy roads along the side of a hill—a la

Dak Pek. This was a Special Forces camp up in the highlands (II Corps) and we only found it by chasing a tortuous river around the cloud covered hills and misty valleys. After off-loading ammunition, mail and rations, we were treated to a Special Forces weapons demonstration and offered a lunch of tiger meat. It seemed that the Green Beret's method of catching a tiger was to wrap a hand grenade in a slab of water buffalo meat, freeze it and put it out for a tiger to come in for a meal. When they heard the explosion, they had fresh tiger meat. I turned down the offer of food, but I took them up on their offer to fire the M-79 grenade launcher. After squeezing off the round, I turned around and said, "That wasn't much". Then the top of the tree at which I had aimed disintegrated with a very loud BANG. I was very impressed with the M-79 but kept my nickel-plated .45 six gun as my weapon of choice.

One such mission was a night resupply of Phuoc Vinh, a Special Forces protected outpost that was under attack by the "Bad Guys". We arrived in the area about 0230 and all seemed quiet from 2500 feet. When we contacted the "Good Guys", they asked us rather emphatically to drop our cargo of .45 caliber, 7.62 millimeter and 81 millimeter mortar ammunition just outside the gate of the fort. They had set up panels for the drop zone leading to the fort and illuminated by truck lights. When "Charlie" shot out the lights of the trucks, we were asked to drop either inside the walls of the fort or just outside the gate. We made several passes up to the fort and actually did get some of the 10 pallets inside the perimeter. Out of the 10 bundles, we managed to get 7 inside, 2 up to the door and no word on where the first one ended up. One reason for the distraction may have been the fact that during our first "orientation" pass, under the meager lighting from the short-lived headlights, a huge tree materialized out of nowhere—looking like a negative—light tree, at eye level, against a black sky. Seconds later, my A/C asked, "Did we miss it?" The only response I could give was, "I still have a wing on my side." Then, all he said was, "Check the fuel tanks, Jacques." The next day, we flew over the fort and there was nothing moving, only a pall of smoke hovering over it. We found out later, that, had we not been there, the fort would have been over run and lost to the "Bad Guys". One unfortunate consequence of the mission was the fact that our door "dropper", who shoved the bundles of ammo out the door, claimed he had been hit by enemy fire and felt that he deserved a Purple Heart. I never saw the wound, so I couldn't back up his claim. The other disappointment was that the crew was turned down for the DFC (Distinguished Flying Cross)—something I have always coveted, but never achieved.

Another of our missions took us to Can Tho down south of Saigon and Bien Hoa, our home base. We discharged our cargo after almost skidding off the muddy PSP runway surface. Looking up to the control tower, we saw that most of the glass was missing or full of holes. Several pieces were leaning up against the tower frame and each one had holes in it and ragged edges. We asked about the cause and the Controller said that they had come under attack. When the friendlies tried to help with helicopter gunships, every time the Controller would talk, the radio panel would light up with a bright green light and the bad guys would put some more rounds through the tower. He was under the console on the floor as the glass was flying. The bad guys (Charlie) were shooting and a couple of UH-1 Hueys were trying to drive them away before they overran the Airfield. We wished we'd been there with a load of flares, but it wasn't our night. However, it was our day to lose a starter on No. 1 engine, so it looked like we had three options: Call back to Bien Hoa for a new starter; try to start the R-1830 with a rope wrapped around the prop shaft and unwind it as fast as a Jeep could pull it; or fix it on-site. We didn't know until the Flight Engineer pulled the back of the starter off that the starter "dog" had broken a ratchet so that it wouldn't engage. By a fantastic stroke of fortune, there was a Filipino mechanic in the Can Tho workshop who was able to build up that broken ratchet with an acetylene torch and a tungsten steel rod. After 2 or 3 hours, as night was approaching, we were able to put the starter dog back on. As the other two options were not going to work out, we cranked up No. 1 just like it should. Since we had never figured a way to "rope start" the engine anyway, plus the fact that the Army didn't even put guards out at night to keep our Gooney Bird from being shot up like the tower, we were very happy to take our leave with many appreciative "Thanks" to our Filipino "savior".

I was required to sit on flare alert several times at Bien Hoa. Usually it was a wasted night just sitting at the Club drinking nothing stronger than Ginger ale. I had found that a jar of olives with the brine removed and replaced with vodka made a long night more pleasant. Since I had been on one flare mission before, I knew what to expect if called out again. At 1200-1500 feet, the flares are at their most effective altitude, set by the flare-throwers in the back. The flares burned at 3000° degrees so they would illuminate quite a large area until burn-out, hopefully near the good guys, not on top of them so they could see the bad guys. One night, we had already dropped about 40 flares, two at a time in case one didn't go off, when I asked the Major Ops Officer in the right seat if we could go around to the right so I could unwind. Since I had already seen the ground fire coming up at us like red basketballs, I wasn't surprised to hear Major Faust exclaim, "Say, Lad, they're shootin' at us up here!" So we climbed 500 feet and the "flare-chuckers" added another 10 seconds to the ignition timing. Regardless of the "brilliant" innovations dreamed up by CAG (Combat Applications Group), the most effective method of dropping any flare was the Loadmaster setting the timing on the fuse and hooking the lanyard to a static line like paratroopers used for jumping, and throwing the flare out the open door. The mechanical devices CAG (Complicated and Garbled) came up with, including metal chutes, compressed air and others, were never as effective as the good old Loadmaster and hand- throwing the flares. One crew had a flare ignite inside the aircraft and the Loadmaster, even though wounded by ground fire and with the C-47 struggling to stay aloft, he was able to grab the burning flare and throw it out the door before it burned through the floor or set off any other flares. For that action, the Loadmaster was awarded the Medal of Honor.

While we were stationed at Bien Hoa, after two new C-47 pilots arrived to augment our resupply missions, we were reassigned to Tan Son Nhut AB in Saigon to fly the VC-47 for 7th Air Force, General Moore and BG Adams. This meant that we were to live in downtown Saigon for a couple of months and fly out of Tan Son Nhut at the whim of the Generals. We had a nice shiny Gooney Bird, silver and white with either 2 blue stars or one blue star under the cockpit window and on the troop door and an American flag on the tail. It had a couch on the starboard side plus airline type seats rather than the fold down troop seats that we'd been used to carrying paratroopers and cargo. Sometimes BG Adams would take the left seat and log C-47 time to keep current. He was a really good pilot, I liked flying with him.

Right after we arrived, we were on our way to the AB when we found out at the gate that a Coup d'Etat was in progress—November 1st 1963. Our first experience with a coup was when we were returning from a resupply mission down south in the delta heading for Bien Hoa. As we approached, with minimum fuel, we beheld a monstrous thunderstorm sitting right over our destination and Bien Hoa was temporarily closed to landings. Therefore, we contacted Tan Son Nhut Tower and requested landing. We were told, "You can land, but no take off!" Since we were so low on fuel, we decided to go ahead and land and see why we "no take off." After touchdown, we were escorted on rollout by two armored personnel carriers (APCs) until we cleared the runway and were ordered at gunpoint to shut down and be searched. After the ARVN Military Police were satisfied that we weren't bad guys, we were allowed to proceed, to the ramp and secured for the night. Then came the hunt for transportation and the answer to what was going on. Evidently, the Vietnam Air Force Commander, Gen. Nguyen Kao Ky, had assumed control of the country and was looking to put down any opposition to his power. Since there were no quarters on base, we had to commandeer a vehicle and venture downtown to find a couple of hotel rooms. After a few wrong turns into barricaded streets with barbed wire and armed soldiers, we made our way to the Majestic Hotel on the Mekong riverfront. When we looked out of our 4th floor window, we saw a Vietnamese Navy LST below us with its 40mm guns pointed directly at our window. There was a great deal of speculation on which side of the coup the Army or the Navy was on. We spent an uneasy night under those Navy guns.

The second coup wasn't nearly as exciting due to its brevity and finality. The reigning Military Commander was a large, cigar-smoking General nicknamed Big Minh. On this morning, he had awakened, gone out on his 2nd floor veranda and saw two tanks in his front yard with their guns pointed right at his bedroom. With no gunfire, the coup was over and I was able to wear a new patch on my hat, "Coup Qualified" with an oak leaf cluster, right under my Airshow Qualified patch.

While we were "luxuriating" in our 4th floor apartment in downtown Saigon, with the flavor of "Nuk Mam" (fermented fish oil) wafting up the stairwell, it came to pass that I should receive my First Pilot check in the VC-47 at Tan Son Nhut. When I repaired for this monumental stage of my piloting career, I was confronted by a 7th AF Check Pilot who had been celebrating something the night before and was obviously a bit hung over. After the mandatory inspection, I was relegated to the left seat to call the checklists and perform all the First Pilot duties while "Zimm" performed the rituals that I had been performing for most of my Gooney Bird career, short though it may have been. At first, the local mission was a normal take off and proficiency check. The check pilot had told me not to fly too low—the ground fire would hurt his head. I remember his words were, "I knew today would be one of those days, because last night was one of those nights." After 15 minutes of maneuvering and Emergency

Procedures, the CP told me to give myself an Instrument Check while he sacked out on the VIP couch in the rear. Following his instructions and not fly low enough to draw any ground fire, I requested an ILS approach back into Tan Son Nhut and awakened my checker so he could observe my instrument approach. He buckled in and gave a big yawn, and decided this was to be a single engine approach with a full stop landing. He pulled No. 2 engine back to simulated failure power, and watched my reaction. With Climb Power on No. 1 engine, flaps at 1/4 and gear down at the Outer Marker, I flew right down the Glide Slope at 90 knots, rounded out at 80 knots and touched down at 70 without a squeak with both engines at idle. As he raised the flaps, all he said was, "Oh, s--t, let's go to the Club and drink beer."—which we did and I passed the check ride. In fact, the final comment by the FE was, "Lt. Jackes is qualified to be up-graded to 1st Pilot in the C-47".

By this time, it was time for R&R since I had flown 50 missions or so resupplying the Special Forces in the field. We had many choices for R&R location, including Hong Kong, Australia and Thailand. I chose Bangkok Thailand as my destination and was able to pick up Pan AM 1 from Saigon to Bangkok. I had heard that a GI could find almost anything he needed there. One thing I needed was a cure for something I had picked up in downtown Saigon— actually, in Cholon, the sleazy part of Saigon where most GIs went to drink Ba-Muy-Ba and get a "Steam and Clean", but you took your life in your hands in the pursuit of cheap fun. There were many Cyclo-races, hangovers and communicable diseases as well as fights and sometimes a night in jail 'til your CO came to bail you out. Most GIs had money to spend and a short time to forget about the war. So, I was off to see the doctor and have fun in Bangkok, eating, sightseeing and buying jewelry.

After checking into the Chao Phraya Hotel, the military billets, on the Chao Phraya River, where everybody in the U S Military stayed when in Bangkok, I had directions to the "storied" Arawan Hotel for dinner and a couple of *Singha* beers. We had a great meal and some wine and just waiting for our dessert. The Arawan had a little club-footed waiter who was part clown and part magician. When one or two U S Military or civilian diners were there, this waiter would put on a performance worthy of a Las Vegas stage. He was particularly renowned for his production of crepe suzettes. He would roll out a cart full of "goodies" and proceed to amaze his audience with bottle flips, plate spins and turns, even with a bad leg, ending up with a flourish of flambé and the words, "Crepe Suzettes, 'Amelican' style".

From there, I made the obligatory trip to James Jewelers. If one wanted to buy jewelry in Bangkok, the military ones went to James. After I climbed the stairs to the expansive showroom the salesman met me, sat me down at a table and asked what I was going to drink. It took an hour and a half, six *Singha*s and over 100 stones before I picked out the "perfect" star sapphire and had it mounted in a white gold ring. I still have that ring, but it no longer has a perfect star after 50 years of abuse in dirt, gravel and rocks.

In 1964, we rotated back to the States on a Military Contract airplane that was crammed full of personnel anxious to get back home. Our first stop out of Saigon was Anchorage Alaska, Elmendorf AFB. We were required to deplane while the aircraft was refueled on the civilian side of the field, since this was a contract operation. We were in summer uniforms and it was rather cool in Alaska, so we headed inside the terminal and straight to the bar on the second floor. There were about 4 or 5 of us in the group and we were all thirsty since nothing alcoholic was served on contract airplanes. After 2 or 3 drinks apiece, our flight was called for re-boarding. Two of the officers in our party were a B-26 pilot and a very cute nurse to whom "Bergie" was being very attentive. They quickly purchased two more martinis and headed downstairs to the departure gate. Bergie had had the forethought to have worn his flight jacket off the airplane, so he concealed both martinis in the pockets of his jacket, walked casually and carefully up the boarding stairs and returned to their seats. After takeoff, the still intact martinis were extracted from their hiding places and surreptitiously consumed without the stewardess noticing a thing. The nurse giggled and I almost applauded.

CHAPTER 8

BACK TO BASICS

Upon our return to Hurlburt, we were considered the most experienced aircrew in all of Air Commando land, in fact, we were chosen as the Tactical Air Command Aircrew of the Quarter. As such, we received a silver cigarette box engraved with the TAC Shield on top and our name engraved with the words, "Outstanding Special Warfare Aircrew, April-June 1964." This was for having trained five new aircrews at Duke Field and exercises like Swift Strike and Cherokee Trail. A lot of our time was spent in North Carolina and as far away as Cannon AFB and Holloman AFB in New Mexico and Homestead AFB in Florida and Watertown New York. One crew we trained in airdrop, short field takeoff and landing became so good, they almost beat us in the "Drop Rodeo" where aircrews had to drop paratroopers and bundles into a small area, the last of which was a 10lb bag of flour to hit a 10ft circle from 100ft altitude at 107 knots airspeed. As soon as they were pronounced "Qualified", they were sent to Bien Hoa to prove it. On one of their first missions, they were returning from Tan Son Nhut AB (Saigon) when an engine caught fire during takeoff. When the Tower notified the crew that one engine was on fire, they started throwing the mail bundles out the troop door as they tried to turn back to the runway. With full power on the other engine, they could see that it was about to fail also. The only recourse was to crash land in a rice paddy, which they did without too much damage to the airplane, but unfortunately, it caused one injury, to the Loadmaster, who was thrown through the latrine door and injured his back. They did everything right, or it could have been a disaster.

One of our training squares to be filled was night, short-field landings without lights on a 3000 foot dirt runway only 75ft wide. My first introduction to this part of the Air Commando syllabus was with a veteran Major who didn't project an air of confidence as far as I was concerned, but after the first approach and landing on the clay strip adjacent to the main runway at Hurlburt and lighted only by eight Combat Controllers with flashlights, it was my turn to try to duplicate this feat of madness, and from the right seat. Fortunately, we had to fly a right-hand pattern at 500ft. I could see the main runway on downwind leg, but upon our radio call turning base leg, the runway lights were extinguished and all I had to look for were two end lights and six "runway" flashlights delineating the runway at 1000 foot intervals. Turning final at 200-300ft, looking at those eight lights was adrenalin-pumping to say the least, but I managed to touch down just before the first pair of lights, raise the flaps and clomp on the "binders" in order to stop in the remaining 2000ft and not run off the end of the runway. Made it! Unfortunately, the Major took over to make the turn around to his left side so we could taxi back for a short-field takeoff, but the 4000 foot remaining marker on the main runway got in the way of our (his) turnaround and the tail collided with the metal marker, effectively shutting down our mission for that night. The short-field takeoff is even more dramatic than the short-field landing—full flaps and the yoke full back until you stall at 55-60 knots. The takeoff procedure is: Brakes tight, Full Power, Yoke forward to lift the tail off and Flaps 15 degrees during the initial roll. At 64 knots, the yoke comes full back and climb at 67 knots to 300 feet with the gear coming up— at 300 feet, you level off, accelerate past Safe Single Engine Speed to 84 knots, raise the flaps, reduce power to METO (Maximum Except Take-Off) and climb out over any obstacles, when you set Climb Power. It is a scary maneuver even in daylight on a hard surfaced runway, but at night, with no lights, on an unprepared runway, it is thrilling, to say the least.

Along with my "Coup Qualified" patch, I earned the not very unique distinction of being "Airshow Qualified", which is a requirement for almost all Air Commandos. Whether you are a flying crewmember with any kind of aircraft in the Flintstone Air Force or a Combat Controller or Combat Weatherman, all of us participated in air shows at one time or another. Whether at Hurlburt, Barksdale, Ft. Bragg or the U.S. Military Academy, we had continual opportunities to show Congressmen, Senators, Foreign Dignitaries or Military Brass how we operated in a Counterinsurgency Theater.

One of our demonstrations involved a "fly-off" between the U-10 Helio Courier and a new turboprop aircraft of similar size and performance. This day was for a demonstration of short field takeoff and landing (STOL) capabilities of the two competing aircraft. Sitting in the stands, erected for this demonstration, was Jimmy Stewart, movie actor and retired Brigadier General. Since both pilots wanted to make a memorable impression on the audience, each had lightened his bird by taking out the right seat, unneeded radios and carrying only minimum fuel. The first demonstrator was an AF Captain in the U-10. He slowed down on final to about 40 knots, crossed the threshold and chopped the power, dropping to the ground with a thud and rolling only about 20 feet. Then he applied full power and was airborne again in about 40 feet. This feat drew much applause and smiles of appreciation. About 3 minutes later, the Turbo Porter, a Swiss-made rescue plane built by Pilatus for high altitude rescue in the Alps, approached the landing zone at about 60 knots. When over touchdown, at about 10 feet, the civilian pilot went into reverse thrust and the Turbo Porter hit the ground with the brakes locked and zero roll out. With power still in reverse he backed up about 10 feet, went to forward thrust with full power and was airborne in about 20 or 30 feet. To really "put the cork in the bottle", the pilot kept the nose raised and made a 360 degree turn into a 15 knot wind and actually backed past the stands before resuming his climb out. He skimmed over the trees and headed for Eglin AFB, just 8 miles away and landed with barely enough fuel with which to taxi in. Needless to say, the applause was even more enthusiastic and the smiles, especially those of the Turbo Porter reps, were very satisfied.

One of the most tragic airshows was a demonstration of the firepower of the B-26, a twin engine fighter bomber with two R-2800 engines and 8 .50 cal. Machine guns in the nose. During a 45 degree bombing or strafing run, the right wing failed and the "old warhorse" that had seen service in WW II, Korea and Vietnam, hit the ground right in front of the Senators and Congressmen watching the show. Fortunately, one of the crewmembers was able to free the other of his seat belt and shove him out the top of the aircraft, just before it hit. He was ejected by the force of the crash, leaving his right leg in the cockpit but he survived also. Right then and there, the B-26 was ordered grounded until a newer version, created by

ONMARK, would be in the Air Commando inventory. The new model had a steerable nose wheel, reversible props, air conditioning/pressurization, and of course, a stronger wing. This was not the first wing failure; there had been one or two in Vietnam, and 4 or 5 crewmembers were lost.

CHAPTER 9

SOS DOESN'T MEAN SAVE OUR SHIP

I would now get a break for 14 weeks for attendance at Squadron Officer School. Before I was due to report in early April, I had time to drive my MG-B to Darlington S.C. to attend the Darlington 500 auto race. I think it was part of the Winston Cup Series at that time. From the infield, with no beer, sleeping under a sports car with the door open so people wouldn't step on me, is not the way to see a major auto race.

While at Squadron Officer School, I had the opportunity to fly the Base Flight C-47 at Maxwell AFB Alabama. Since I had many hours in it, I was considered Aircraft Commander Qualified which meant I could fly with un-qualified Co-pilots. Therefore, I became an Instructor to a couple of jet-jockeys, F-100 pilots, and was very eager to show these "fast-movers" just what the old Gooney Bird could do and the way the Air Commandos do it. So, for my first act, I taxied out to the grass overrun on the active runway and proceeded to brief one of the "Lead Sled" (F-100) pilots how we were going to take off in less than 1000 feet, how to put down 1/4 flaps, hold the throttles at Max Power and how to unlock and raise the gear after lift-off while I was climbing to 300 feet. If we lost an engine before 300 feet, we would try to get the gear back down, while shutting down the affected engine, etc., etc.

With the brakes locked, full power on the 1830s and the control yoke full back, we started the take-off roll. At 60 knots, with the yoke forward now, I called for quarter flaps and as we hit 67 knots, Minimum Flying Speed, I hauled the nose up to 15 degrees and called: "Gear Up!" We accelerated to 84, Minimum Safe Single-Engine Speed, and I leveled off at 300 feet, called for METO Power and continued to climb as I called for After Take-off Checklist. The jet-jock couldn't believe that we were still airborne and that we had used only 700 feet of runway.

For my next act, I proceeded to show them that I could land in the same distance, so I slowed to 84 knots, gear down, full flaps and aimed for the end of the runway just short of the numbers. With power on and nose low, I rolled it on the first 100 feet, power off, flaps up and tail down. We stopped even without maximum braking just before the first runway remaining marker. All the way down final approach, the Co-pilot was pushing back in his seat, gaping at the Airspeed Indicator without a 1 in front of the

67 knots indicated.

A couple of years later, I had the chance to fly in the back seat of an F-100D at Homestead AFB in Florida with a cool jet-jockey on a range mission on Avon Charlie Gunnery Range, upon which I had dropped lots of flares the night before. In the back seat of the F-100 I could see very little forward except the back of Jim Manion's ejection seat. As we started takeoff roll, he told me that I was going to make the two-ship formation takeoff with the Squadron Commander on our right wing. What a kick when the afterburner kicked in and as soon as we broke ground and the gear was coming up, the Colonel on the wing became lead, as I found out later, was his favorite position anyway, so Jim took over to follow his boss to Avon Charlie for bombing and gunnery practice. Once we established our pattern over the range, we began our first bomb run, a 45° degree dive angle approach to the bull's eye target. In the back seat, I had my little Minolta pocket-sized camera ready to take pictures of the event. I was ready to take the shot when our practice bomb cleared and we started a 4G pull-out at about 400 knots. The camera now felt like it weighed about 12 pounds as we pulled up to a downwind perch. I recovered my camera from between my knees in time to look down at the target. "Did we hit it?" he asked and all I could see was a small white cloud of smoke somewhere near the center, but not real close. From that moment on, it was roll in for 30°, 10° and 0° degree bomb runs plus a couple of gun runs until we were "Winchester", out of ammo. Evidently, we had a slight problem with directional control, because the F-100 kept jerking right and left during the run-in to the target. The pilot kept cursing and jamming the rudder to counter the "jinking" right or left, I couldn't tell which. (The STAB AUG, or Stabilizer Augmentation, was not functioning properly). The last gun run, with the 20mm cannons chattering, at 320 knots and 100 feet with the nose jerking back and forth, was a truly memorable experience for a low/slow pilot like me. I guess it was retribution for "showing my stuff" to those jet-jockeys at Squadron Officers School.

Dropping flares on Avon Charlie Gunnery Range turned out to be more of a challenge than usual due to the strong winds across the range at 90 degrees to the target run-in heading. We dropped our first two flares as the first F-100 descended from its 5000 feet "perch". Both the flares and the F-100 were drifting off the target line so that we never saw the target and had to move our pattern 500 feet up-wind, then 1000 feet because the flares were about to set fires off the range. The wind must have been about 25-30 knots from the right. With the F-100s flying a right-hand pattern, we were inside their run-in and pull-up to downwind. After the first F-100 passed between our wing and the tail of our flare bird and the Loadmaster heard it dive past us, we called a halt to the proceedings and took a break. Following a tactical discussion on the ground about pattern position of the C-47 vis-à-vis the jet fighters, we improvised a pattern from the opposite side in order to stay out of the F-100 pattern, but the co-pilot had to call when to drop the flares from the right-hand side. That way we stayed out of each other's way and didn't set any more fires.

We had an Intelligence NCO who had an unusual pet which he decided to bring along with him on a mission to North Carolina on my C-47. We were on our way to yet another joint exercise for which the Air Force Commander decided he needed to have an Intel-type on his staff. This particular TSgt had a very German or Dutch name like Van Ryke or Van Rycke as I recall. He was standing by the entry stairs checking on something already loaded on the Gooney Bird. When I followed his gaze up under the troop seats, I saw two rather intense, unblinking eyes staring back in the gloom of the shady cabin. I recoiled slightly and asked the obvious question, to which he replied, "That's my pet mountain lion, he has two Demerol in him and doesn't know where he is." After a 4 hour flight, the mountain lion had awakened and when I saw the TSgt, his feet were leaving the door on the other end of the straightened leash trying to stay up-right as his pet headed for the trees. That was the last time I saw either of them.

From our home base of Hurlburt, we were allowed to practice low-level infiltration and exfiltration practice missions flying at treetop level over long and ever-changing routes through northern Florida and southern Alabama. During these low-level treks, I was flying an HC-47. I not only had twice the fuel as a normal C-47, I also had loudspeakers mounted in the cargo door and two wooden ADF antennas hanging from each wing near the tip. As we approached our next turning point, the Navigator said to turn over the bridge spanning a nice quiet lake, so I merely banked enough to make the left turn while dragging the two ADF antennas in the water. I asked the Navigator to come up and look to see if I was turning correctly. When he saw the wingtip a foot above the water and the antennas leaving a wake behind us he could scarcely mutter something about "crazy" or "dangerous" as he slipped back to his seat and buckled his belt and harness. Later on during that mission, we hooked up with 2 T-28 escorts which were for simulated ground fire suppression in the drop area. Before the T-28s settled in on our wing, we saw a cotton field ahead that looked like something out of <u>Gone With The Wind</u>. There were 3 or 4 black "mammies" hoeing or picking cotton. They heard us coming upon them at almost eye level, picking up dust with our props. They turned to face us and fell over backwards right down in the cotton rows. After we passed, they started to get up and here came one T-28, followed at 100 feet by another T-28. Back down they went, probably with a couple of "Lordies!"

Following that, we simulated our drop and, still at 50-75 feet altitude, we started for home on our ex-filtration route. The next person we saw down in the bare field below was a tall, slender black boy of about 15, shirtless, and with three brothers and sisters tagging along behind him. My Navigator had also seen them and had turned on the power to the ALTEC Speakers. When that black boy saw us, he reached down and picked up a big clod of dirt, "rared back" and was going to throw it at us as we passed by. Jerry hit the mike button and exclaimed, "DON'T YOU THROW THAT ROCK, BOY!" Man, he dropped that thing like it was radioactive and, when last seen, he was three shades lighter and headin' for home with all three of his brothers and sisters behind him. I always wondered what he told his mother about that.

When we were sent out to Cannon AFB in New Mexico, we were to drop flares on Oscura Range, elevation 9500 feet. This "exercise" was for the F-100s of the 481st Fighter Squadron—the "Green Crusaders". Since the missions were all at night and required us to drop flares for their gunnery and bomb runs, we were dropping from about 11,000-12,000 feet, not too high an altitude for a jet, but somewhat fatiguing for an old recip and crew. During the break between range missions, usually around 9:30 or 10:00, the F-100s would return to Cannon to refuel and rearm, leaving us to either "loiter" at 11,000 feet for an hour and a half or, my favorite choice, fly south for 15 or 20 minutes and land at Holloman AFB, eat, hydrate and spend some time with a cute little nurse. She lived in the permanent party BOQ (Bachelor Officers Quarters) and she always had Johnny Carson on and a comfy couch. That made that 0100 mission easier to stay up for. Unfortunately, the F-100s, after completing their mission would "race" back to Cannon, leaving us to straggle back home at 1/4 of their speed. By the time we arrived within sight of Cannon, the Base, and certainly the Tower, was ready to shut down. The first night, we called the Tower and requested landing. With no response, we called on Guard Channel (243.0) and heard, "Who is this?" I grabbed the mike and said, "This is your flare ship—how about letting us land?"

The next day, we departed at about 7 PM and followed our route due West into the setting sun. Upon setting Climb Power, but deciding that we didn't need that much power, I eased back to just enough to maintain a 100-200 feet per minute climb over the gently rising terrain. Even squinting into the setting sun, I could see herds of sheep grazing less than 100 feet below us, so—why not do a little sheep-herding at 100 knots and 50-75 feet? What fun watching them scatter!

During a subsequent mission to Holloman, we were resupplying Guerillas in the Sacramento Mountains at night. The drop signal for this night was an inverted "C" and as we flew our prescribed course to the drop site, we looked and looked in the darkness for our signal. As the drop time came and went, we suddenly noticed what looked like our signal to the right about a half mile away, so I told the Loadmaster to drop our bundles on the green light. After the last bundle was out the door, the Navigator yelled, "Pull up and turn left!" At 10,000 feet, the old Gooney Bird didn't want to move up too quickly. As we climbed away and headed back to base, we all breathed a sigh of relief. The next day, my nurse friend and I drove up to Cloudcroft Resort on top of one of the Sacramento peaks—a beautiful, scenic place with a view of the whole valley and desert. As we were having a drink in the bar, I was telling about our previous night's drop mission and how we had to suddenly pull up and climb above 10,000 feet to clear the terrain. The waitress overheard, and said, "Was that YOU? You flew right past the dining room window at eye level. We could see the flames coming out of your stacks!" We must have scared the peacocks to death and I don't know how we missed the flag pole. To put the frosting on the cupcake, we found out when we returned to Holloman, that instead of dropping rations to the "Guerillas", we had actually dropped cases of C-Rations into a Girl Scout camp which had arranged its fires in an inverted C pattern.

Upon our return to base, (RTB in fighter language), we had only a day or two off. Due to my familiarity with the C-47 assigned to Maxwell AFB, (remember Squadron Officer School), I was tasked to go back to pre-flight C-47 #49038 and bring it to Hurlburt as a "Re-assignment Asset". When we arrived at Hurlburt, the maintenance crews went to work installing 10 .30 caliber machine guns in that old bird—2 in each of the last 3 windows and 4 in the troop door. Then, while I was out "talking to the trees" with loudspeakers as training for the Psychological Operations (Psy Ops) program, other aircrews were checking out "Puff the Magic Dragon" on Eglin AFB gunnery ranges. Unfortunately, the old .30 calibers, after many range missions, burned out with age and overuse since WW II. Therefore, some brilliant planner devised the 7.62 mm Gattling Gun from General Electric and the legend was born. The <u>Air Commando Journal</u> of Summer 2012 recreates the history on "SPOOKY, SPECTRE and the MAN—How the AC-47 Gunship Came to Be".

But instead of "Puff the Magic Dragon" I was relegated to the realm of Psychological Welfare and for the next two years. I became one of the leaders of the "Bullshit Bombers"—dropping leaflets (and sometimes toilet paper) and "talking to the trees" with loudspeakers.

On Sundays at Hurlburt, some of us would spend a good part of the day at the O. Club, which had actually been built by Al Capone for a summer house, a quiet retreat from the Prohibition Era complexities of Chicago. It was located on the Inland Waterway and had a dock to which many boat-owners would tie up on Sunday to spend a day eating freshly-shucked oysters and drinking whatever. By the time 6 or 7 boatloads had tied up and were crowded into the bayside bar, the crowd would overwhelm the black "Oyster

Shucker" in the back bar by the time the 9th or 10th dozen was ordered. The last time I saw him, he had thrown down his gloves and apron in the direction of the bartender and was heading out the back door, muttering something like, "I ain't doin' this no mo'!" He was probably making $2.50 or less an hour, since it was 1964. I really couldn't blame him. With many war stories, funny anecdotes, sexist jokes, flirting and much drinking, the day would drag on to dinner time and, since nobody wanted to go home and cook, we always planned on making it to the dining room, but seldom made it. The 4 or 5 of us would usually say, "Oh, just one more and then we'll go eat." By the last round, the dining room had closed and we would all go home hungry, and drunk. In those days, I was usually hanging around with Hank Hendry, my 2nd Aircraft Commander in Vietnam and his wife Fay, and George Lattin, my A/C in Greenwood S.C., and his wife Kay, Fay's twin sister, "The beautiful Sisters Flower from Petal Mississippi" as I called them. I knew Fay (don't ask) better than Kay so I could always tell them apart, even skinny-dipping in the surf at the Eglin Beach Club one Friday night. (And that's the name of that tune.)

One aspect of the Psy War program was to fly low level missions to hide the location of our destination or target, and either drop leaflets or use the loudspeakers to broadcast messages in English, Spanish or Vietnamese. One day, I was heading to Hurlburt or the O. Club when I was flagged down on Hwy 98 by an AP (Air Police) car. I was pulled over and was informed that I had 2 hours to pack up and return to the Squadron for a 30 day mission. There was no clue where it was to be or what it was to be, but I made it in time for the pre-mission briefing. One hour later, with props turning, bags loaded, navigation charts spread out modes and codes copied, clearance on request and take off and departure briefed, we saw the Wing Commander standing alongside the runway waving adieu after promising we would be back in a month or so, or as soon as possible. So, after a right turn out of traffic, we were on our way to a new adventure—a somewhat classified one, about which we were not too knowledgeable—but off we went.

The first stop was Homestead AFB for fuel, overwater briefing and survival equipment. Then we were off to Ramey AFB Puerto Rico to receive further guidance as to what we were doing there and what was in store for the future. One unexpected glitch had already been overcome when we crossed the ADIZ (Air Defense Identification Zone). In response to our position report and estimate to the ADIZ, we found out that our classified call sign had changed due to its expiration at the end of the month. It was only 1700 local time, but it was 2400 Zulu (Greenwich Mean Time, or GMT) in England which meant that our call sign had to change to the new month. It also meant that we were unknown to Air Traffic Control until we found our new call sign. Having breached that obstacle, we landed at Ramey and prepared to enjoy the rest of the evening. However, in the middle of a lobster tail and a bottle of Rose, I received word that we were due at San Isidro in the Dominican Republic that very night, so we collected ourselves and headed northwest.

Once we finally found San Isidro AB, we contacted the US Control Team and were allowed to land. However, nobody seemed to know who we were, where we were to shut down or where we were going to base our operations. The first night was a madhouse of securing a parking space, a 6-man tent and a place to pitch our "camp". Our crew was relegated to a patch of grass adjacent to the south ramp which contained several British aircraft in various states of disrepair over which we pitched our tent. That first night was every man for himself to find a place to lay out our sleeping bags beside the "Douglas Hilton". I chose the horizontal stabilizer of an old single engine, twin boom British jet which I had propped up with wooden blocks so I wouldn't roll off onto the ground 5 or 6 feet below me as I did once before the bracers were in place to hold the stabilizer in the nose up position. With some degree of urgency, we had the local Marine Detachment build a wooden floor so we would be off the ground.

Our mission there was called "Operation Vivres". It entailed dropping leaflets all over the countryside in the Dominican Republic telling all who found them or heard our broadcasts from our huge loudspeakers that the current government was trying to make their lives better and was not going to be over thrown. At least, I think that is what we were doing—everything was in Spanish. We had to fly to Roosevelt Roads NAS to pick up Spanish-speaking Marines to deliver our loudspeaker messages.

In order to deliver our leaflets more efficiently, which meant having them land just where we wanted, CAG (remember "Complicated and Garbled?) had come up with a high altitude delivery system that entailed tying bundles of paper with primer cord with a plastic cone on the bottom so that the bundle would fall straight until the burning primer cord separated at low altitude and released the leaflets. Since the delivery system needed to be tested in the theater, we spent half a day dropping leaflet bundles from 5-7000 feet trying to hit the mouth of the Ozama River near Santo Domingo. Of course, that meant that all the leaflets that <u>did</u> manage to hit the river or blew out to sea, had to be policed up by the U.S. Navy off shore. They were not too happy about being on clean-up duty instead of seeing some action. Our "action" consisted of explaining to the Air Attaché why we were parked on his pad and abiding the Spanish-speaking Marines, who were actually Dominican soldiers or Puerto Rican, I was never sure which, who had joined the USMC. Anyway, they kept things lively while we were on the ground. One evening, our Flight Engineer was changing the heat exchanger on No. 1 engine with our help—holding a flashlight and handing up a "bigger hammer" when two of our borrowed Marines came roaring up the ramp to our position and exclaimed, "Look what we found!" Then they handed us two or three small bottles of Dominican Rum from their cache inside their jackets and sped off. Somehow, we managed to replace the offending heat exchanger despite the consumption of most of the rum, then we hit the sack.

Most of our missions with loudspeaker and/or leaflets were uneventful. However, one evening we were flying a support mission for the Ambassador whose agent had briefed us on the area to be covered. Then he and a high-ranking Officer took off in their own plane while we were left to drop leaflets, not from 5-7000 feet, but at house top level over Santo Domingo itself. We had flown similar missions before with "advisors" on board, which must have been boring for them, but this night, we were all by ourselves. After a few passes around the outskirts, we started a roof top pass down an almost deserted street as the daylight was fading. There was enough daylight to see a camouflaged Che Guevera look-a-like in a Jeep cock his Thompson 45 cal. machine gun and let loose with a stream of bullets which we couldn't avoid from 100 feet and 120 knots. Just as the first ones hit, my co-pilot closed his plexiglass window next to him and froze in his seat. After the "thump, thump, thump" quit and we were out of range, I told him, "You can come out now, he's quit shooting." We had taken 8 or 9 rounds through the floor but the only souvenir we could find after landing was one slug that ended up in the bottom of the Boss's hang-up bag. The airplane could have received a Purple Heart, but all I received was an Overseas Expeditionary Forces Medal and a hangover from Dominican Rum.

We were wondering how long our "week or two" was going to last and how we were going to put up with the "General Restrictions" that had been imposed by the reigning "powers that be"—including, having to wear a weapon in order to be admitted to the chow hall on site. Since we hadn't brought our personal weapons with us, we had to use the M-16s that had been issued to us aircrew members in a "hostile environment" when we deployed. One of our 2nd Lieutenants in charge of our Psy Ops broadcasts and leaflet drops, an Army "puke", but a pleasant one, didn't "cotton" to such an order, but when he entered our tent, someone hit him chest high with an M-14, which almost knocked him back out of the tent. From then on, we all carried our sidearms.

When flying out of Hurlburt, usually to the West and Northwest, there were many occasions when the weather played a decisive role. One day, we were scheduled for some kind of training mission to a destination in Texas, or somewhere in that direction. When I checked the enroute weather, the Base Meteorologist summed our chance of success with a terse comment, "If the freezing rain doesn't get you, the tornados will!" That was an automatic CNX WX, Cancelled Weather in shorthand abbreviations. During a subsequent mission to Kansas, we were chugging along to the Northwest and we started to pick up cumulus clouds, a little rain and moderate turbulence. As it became more and more difficult to control the aircraft in straight and level flight, I was finally able to have the co-pilot catch the microphone and call Little Rock Center, relay our position and request clearance back to home base. It wasn't easy to wrestle our Douglas "Racer" around to a reciprocal heading and smoother flying for the two hour trip back to England AFB. During the post-mission debriefing and explanation of our abort, we learned that a tornado had just touched down in Texarkana Texas, right near where we had turned around. That had almost become a permanent CNX WX.

The trip down to Mission Texas seemed like a milk-run, just taking some officers down to the tip of the state to look at their investment properties in the orange/grapefruit orchards on the Rio Grande River. Since it was a civilian airfield with no weather station, we relied on our pre-mission weather briefing that mentioned the possibility of a cold front passing by us on our way back, but I thought we would be back in time to avoid any problems associated with a wind shift and a temperature drop. By the time our passengers were through with their tour, the front had already crossed our homeward bound route. All we could do was press on home and hope we wouldn't have any problems. About 50 miles out of England, we started to pick up some icing, so I, in the right seat, applied carburetor heat by pulling back the two levers in front of me on the instrument panel/console. With a D-model C-47, the engine nacelles had a sand screen installed in the air scoop that closed off the airflow from the front of the air scoop and redirected through the screen at the rear of the nacelle if you pull the levers all the way to the stop. Since we didn't need the screens, just the heat, I pushed the levers out of the full back detent, so we would just have heat, but the right engine carb heat lever would not come out of the detent, no matter how hard I pushed, jiggled and tried to bend the right lever. The result was icing of the screen, gradually shutting off the airflow to No. 2 engine. The A/C added power to the left engine as the right one wound down to a stop and had to be feathered to reduce drag. We declared an emergency, informed the passengers of our problem and landed safely on one engine. I was still trying to force the lever out of the detent, so we could restart No. 2 and taxi in under our own power. Fortunately, it was Sunday afternoon and with no other inbound traffic, we were able to ease right off the runway and call for a tug, while a bus was dispatched to off load our passengers. When Maintenance looked into the problem after I had finally and easily repositioned the lever to forward position, they found that a bolt that was too long had been installed at some time or another and that had locked the lever in the down position. That sure made me feel better that it wasn't all my fault.

One particular mission not involving a Field Training Exercise, loudspeakers or leaflets was a quick trip to Miami, FLA to deliver one of our C-47s to Miami Airways for IRAN, Inspect and Replace-As- Necessary. It was kind of a milk run, just fly it down, turn it in for maintenance and return via commercial air to England AFB, La. As we approached Ft. Meyer VORTAC, we called Miami Approach Control for landing at Miami Intl. Since we were still some 80 to 100 miles out Approach Control kind of forgot about us as we approached at 120 knots. Finally, after about ten minutes, and 20 miles of progress, we were asked, "What is your airspeed?" I replied, "One hundred and twenty." "Oh, wow, could you increase that a little?" "Yeah, we could go to 130" Their final response was "You're cleared for ILS RWY 09 L, report outer marker inbound to Tower on 118.1" This kind of perturbed Jerry in the A/C position. With the runway in sight about 25 miles ahead, we were already on final approach, so he said" Gear Down" and we began the Before Landing Checklist. As our airspeed decreased, he called for Flaps 1/4, then Flaps ½. By now, we could see commercial airliners lining up on the taxiway for takeoff. When we came to the outer marker, I called Tower on 118.1, but all we heard was "Yeah, he sure is! If you want to complain, call (some telephone number)." We continued our full flap approach at Air Commando short field speed of 69 knots, touched down in the first 300 feet and turned off at the first taxiway. Immediately thereafter, it rained airliners out of Miami International, but we were still chuckling.

Now, we had to make it back to Alexandria. We had a flight scheduled to New Orleans on Delta or something, and then we were to take Southern, "Sudden", as we called it, from there to Alex. The airline check-in folks were a little miffed that we were checking through two parachutes, but we assured them that it wasn't because we were afraid of flying, just regulation for aircraft delivery. I had called the Motor Pool at England AFB for transportation from Essler Field to the base, so we headed north on a DC-3 even older, possibly, then the one we had just left in Miami. Since I was curious about the cockpit layout, I asked the Stewardess if I could come up front for a visit. She looked confused and began her litany, "FAA Regulations prohibit---passengers from—uh, uh- "I just said I knew what she was trying to tell me and sat down where I obviously belonged.

Upon arrival at Essler Field, 7 or 8 miles across the river in Pineville, there was no transportation waiting to take us and our gear back to England AFB so we could turn our chutes. I called again and found out that a shift change had fouled up the request, but that they could be there in about half an hour. Instead, we found a kindly soul who was driving a nice Cadillac and was heading that way, so we threw our gear in the trunk and off we went. During the ride back, our chauffeur remarked about how "provincial" Alexandria was, with its cobblestone streets and even gas lights. He said he didn't even borrow money in the state, that unless you were a Couvillion, a Gremillion or a

Bergeron, you didn't have a chance of borrowing. He went all the way to Texas instead.

Upon our return to Miami International, we were dropped off this time and unable to "terrorize" the outbound jet traffic, so we could return our newly renovated Gooney Bird to England AFB. However, during my walk-around, I found that the restraining straps in the wheel wells had steel brake pads designed to stop the tires spinning at 85 to 90 MPH. This C-47 was equipped with steel cord tires made especially for landing on snow (a la Watertown) or on muddy landing strips (a la Can Tho). If those steel cord tires were to rub against the steel brake pads, a shower of sparks would inundate the wheel wells and possibly cause a fire. We called for maintenance personnel to come out and replace the steel pads with brass ones. It was lunch break, so we had to wait until the Brake Pad Specialist could be rounded up and sent out to us sitting on the hot ramp trying to keep cool under the wing of our ride home. Over one hour later, this non-English-speaking Cuban towed his little red tool cart and eight brass brake pads out to our position and did his job. It reminded me of my criticism of specialized maintenance: "Will the Standby C-47 Aileron Trim Tab Dope and Fabric Man please report to the flight line?" After another 45 minutes, we had to find a supervisor who was qualified to sign off the write-up and we were finally on our way. Now it was Miami Ground Control's turn to get even with this non-jet intruder. We would just have to wait until there was no more outbound traffic. We could have eaten a much better lunch had we known how long it would take. "Touche" Miami.

CHAPTER 10

BACK TO FUN AND GAMES

Now it was time to return to Vietnam and exercise our capabilities with speaker and leaflet. Four aircrews were designated to become the 5th Air Commando Squadron, Psychological Warfare experts with 4 C-47s equipped with loudspeakers. How to get them over to Vietnam? We had to fly as a 4-ship formation from Hurlburt AFB FL to Nha Trang RVN via California, Alaska, Midway, Wake Island, Guam, the Philippines and eventually, Nha Trang. When we arrived at our destination, again, nobody knew what to do with us or where to put us, but, being resourceful and somewhat desperate, we found our own place for our airplanes as well as aircrews.

The trip across the "Big Pond" was long, but occasionally exciting. Our first stop was Sacramento, California, Mc Clellan AFB, from which I had flown WB-50s until 1963. We arrived at too late an hour for any reunions due to the fact that we were flying an HC-47, a rescue type Gooney Bird with two extra 400 gallon fuel tanks and dump valves so we had 1600 gallons of fuel vs 800 for the others which meant we could fly non-stop from Hurlburt to Mc Clellan by way of San Diego, not exactly the "Crow Flight Route".

GOOD OL' GOONEY BIRDS - My favorite airplane, the C-47. This is an HC-47, modified for long range Air Search and Rescue with extra 400 gallon fuel tanks outboard of the engines with dump values under the wings to rid the plane of almost 5000 lbs. of fuel in an emergency. At 2 miles a minute to Vietnam, we

logged 85 hours – so the trip was 10,200 miles, or almost halfway around the world.

It took us 16 hours and 5 minutes to fight headwinds the whole way. At one point, there were cars on Route 66 that were passing us up. We even entered a mountain wave, winds strong enough coming over the Rockies and down upon us with such force that we had to apply Climb Power just to keep our airspeed above the stall and maintain altitude. I actually saw a red sports car on the Interstate we were following pass us up a couple of times. When we turned north from San Diego to complete our first leg of our trip to Vietnam, we had been in the air for half a day. I had almost forgotten how to land at Mc Clellan at about 10:30 PM with the three hour time change. After receiving our initial briefing from the 4440th Aircraft Delivery Group, to whom we now belonged, we were off to the great unknown. We were supposed to pick a call sign for our 4 aircraft and I wanted to pick "Six foot—one, two, three and four." However, I was overruled and due to our overall mission designation, we had to use the call sign of "Quick Speak." I think that was the opportunity to check on my old homestead on Layton Drive just outside the North Gate. When I found a ride with one of the Permanent Party members of the 4440th ADG, before we had to depart for our next leg of our trip, the first thing I noticed about our cute little green and white house was that it was now two-toned brown. I recalled having told my sweet tenant that if she bought the paint, she could repaint the house, but there is only one description for those two shades of brown, and it's both dirty and smelly. I never have found out if it was repainted to its original color after I finally sold it for a big loss, since the FHA declared that area to be "depressed". Not good for home sales.

Our first (second?) leg to the orient wasn't to be WSW to Honolulu (Hickam AFB) since the winds were -5, five knots on the nose against us, so we were rerouted up to Alaska, to Elmendorf AFB at Anchorage. Since I had spent 3 years flying WB-50s out of Eielson AFB in Fairbanks, Alaska was like home to me. But we were on a schedule mandated by the 4440th ADG which meant 14 hours on the ground, then off to the west for leg three all the way out to Adak. Since Quick Speak 2 had lost radio contact on the way out to the end of Alaska, the Boss decided he should turn back with 2 and return to Elmendorf, leaving John Lee, Quick Speak 3, and me to press on out to the murky cold of the Aleutian Chain. Adak NAS is about as far away from the "Lower 48" civilized world as one can get and still be part of the U S Military. The weather kept getting more miserable the farther out on the Chain we went. By the time we were in radio contact with Adak Approach Control the weather was in the weeds. The ceiling was down to 300-400 feet and forecast to go below minimums at any time, so I went in first. A pilot—Naval Aviator—ahead of me declared the ceiling was right on minimums and going down, but I found the approach lights in and out of the fast-moving clouds and put my Gooney Bird on the ground. When Approach Control asked me if it should close the field, I knew John Lee was approaching right behind me, so I told them it was still above minimums—200 feet and one mile visibility. Right after John landed I agreed to tell the truth, that indeed Adak was now below minimums and the field was closed as we were taxiing in and shut down.

More excitement to follow—the next destination was Midway Island—appropriately, about half way to our final destination of Nha Trang, S. Vietnam. When we arrived, it was Gooney Bird season and the entire island was covered while outdoors with nesting Gooney Birds. The airplane we were flying obtained its nickname from the fact that Gooney Birds (seagull relatives) are rather ungainly when struggling to take off, but very graceful after they are airborne. However, they have a similar awkwardness upon landing, usually falling over upon touchdown but able to recover quickly. So it is with the C-47 if not handled properly. Our stay on Midway was memorable, not only for our need to watch every step we made to avoid stepping on a nesting Gooney Bird, but for me, it was memorable because someone stole my hat, made in Vietnam, the official Air Commando hat with the plastic covered pink silk lining and snap brim on one side. The original 1963 version was hard to come by unless you found one at the Officers Club at Midway and stole it.

By the time we had spent a night avoiding stepping

on clucking Gooney Birds, we were ready to press on with our own two engine Gooney Bird to our next landing spot further across the ocean—Wake Island. Upon feeling the wind blowing 20-25 knots on our way to Base Operations, we prudently and necessarily checked the weather for our route west to Wake, but the local weather loomed as our biggest problem. With the barometer falling and the wind rising, it appeared, that if we didn't move soon, immediately, if not sooner, we would be stuck on Midway while a typhoon passed over it and probably scattering the avian Gooney Birds as well. Since I'd seen enough of Midway and being an Air Weather Service alumnus, I made the decision to "go for the bold" and head west as soon as we could crank up our C-47s and be cleared for takeoff. John was a bit reluctant to try to outrun an approaching typhoon, but having flown for Air Weather Service for 3 ½ years, I knew more about weather than he did so I convinced him that we would be running away from the cyclone, if we could only get off the runway and turn west. Therefore, I told him to strap that Gooney Bird on his ass and follow me. I also told the tower to give me the wind direction and speed every few minutes as we taxied out and when it was within 35 degrees of the runway heading and less than 30 knots, we would have our max crosswind component and could take off. After about 10 minutes at the end of the runway, the tower told us we had our proper component and away we went. I could see blue sky on the western horizon and 20 minutes after takeoff, we were in the clear and on our way to Wake Island. On the inter-plane frequency John asked me "What would we have done if I'd been wrong?" I could only answer, "I wasn't".

By the time our 2-plane element arrived at Wake Island, we had been heading west in a 2-engine airplane over a 4-engine ocean for four straight days so, after we shut down and de-planed, we were met by the local representative of the 4440th Aircraft Delivery Group who was a Major and had our flight plan, weather briefing, flight lunch request, refueling, etc., all ready for the next day's departure. When I informed him that I intended to rest a day and let the other two airplanes catch up to us, I was informed in no uncertain terms that the next day we were to be off at 0800 local time and our next stop would be Anderson AFB Guam. He also informed me that we were not yet the 5th Air Commando Squadron, and that we still belonged to the 4440th until we landed at Nha Trang RVN.

Well, when we arrived at Anderson AFB, I had had enough of the 4440th ADG and found a few ways to amuse myself on Guam, ignoring the protocol of aircraft delivery, I enjoyed an evening and night drinking, playing miniature golf, drinking, eating and trying to find any other form of diversion without ever considering the prospect of another two days of "pressing on" to arrive in Vietnam. I kind of remember a bottle of bourbon, a fellow crewmember, a Flight Mechanic I believe (I also believe his name was Bender) and finishing said bottle. The next thing I remember is using a mop in Base Ops on the marble floor. Following that fleeting insight into my overall condition, the next thing I remember is waking up on a stretcher in my C-47 and asking, "Who's flying this thing?" I was informed that it was one of our T-28 pilots accompanying us to Vietnam. When I finally took over the flying duties we were only a little more than an hour out of Clark AFB, and Dick Hildreth was more than willing to relinquish the left seat after having spent over 8 ½ hours in it—a long time for a single engine pilot—but I was glad that he had had some previous C-47 experience. I never did find out how he happened to be in command but it was most likely the work of the 4440th, plus he outranked me and my co-pilot. After landing at Clark AFB, we made our way to the Billeting Office and were informed that the only transient aircrew overnight accommodations were almost off-base in an area containing a couple of dozen trailers used for overflow billeting. Even though this seemed like an inconvenience we shouldn't have to suffer, I had noticed a sign in the office that proclaimed that beer was available for purchase right there at the counter. The heck with the inconvenience, just sell me a couple of *San Miguels*—some say the best beer in the World. I didn't know about its World status, it certainly seemed to be the best beer I had ever had.

The next leg of our long journey was also our last one, from Clark AFB to Nha Trang. Since we still comprised only one half of the 5th Air Commando Squadron, we were uncertain as to what our reception would be like upon our arrival "in-country". Evidently, nobody at Nha Trang knew either. Nobody knew who we were or why we were there much less where to put us. So, we were on our own until the other half with the boss arrived to straighten things out. So we managed to secure parking spots for our tired C-47s and quarters for our tired aircrew members at the Pacific Hotel with our Flight Orders that showed Nha Trang RVN as our final destination. Then, we waited to find out what was to come next.

Having finally traversed the same ocean we had just crossed, Major Cresse and the other crews arrived and took charge of our Psychological Warfare missions. Our job was to drop leaflets and deliver loudspeaker messages trying to urge the VC to give up their quest to take over all of South Vietnam for the Communists. The leaflets were very colorful—lots of red—graphic—lots of dead VC bodies—and gruesome messages, unintelligible to us, were delivered over our large speakers mounted in the cargo door and leaning out in the slipstream pointing toward the ground from about 1000 to 1500 feet. Our motto, at least mine, was, "The rain in the plain may mainly spoil their aim". But I found out the hard was that that wasn't true. Along with that lesson, I learned not to fly a predictable pattern when delivering our loudspeaker message. After orbiting for about 45 minutes over 2 or 3 towns with our ALTECHS blaring along a rather large road as it curved to the south, the VC decided to put a stop to our program. All of a sudden, it sounded like we had run into a hail storm with .30 caliber rounds coming through the fuselage. I heard the little Vietnamese girls scream and huddle together while I rolled sharply right and headed for the nearest airfield. Nobody claimed any injury, but the airplane had obviously taken some hits. After landing at Tuy Hoa, I jumped off the backdoor step like a paratrooper and started looking for battle damage. As I was poking my finger into 3 or 4 holes I could reach, a platoon of ARVN soldiers had asked me as soon as I hit the ground, "You go 'Na Chang', you go' Na Chang'?" While they watched me examine the holes around and under the fuselage, the trailing Vietnamese soldiers started jabbering excitedly and, after looking at a hole about the size of my hand right under the co-pilot's elbow, I saw the whole ARVN platoon heading in formation off to look for another way to "Na Chang". I looked up at the co-pilot and told him to stay put, turn on the mag switches and fuel selector and get ready to roll. I told him he didn't even want to see the hole on his side until we got home. Fortunately, we didn't have any ARVN soldiers to carry with us, just two scared Vietnamese girls.

Life at Nha Trang was a bit like a vacation at the beach. Even though we were advised that if we wanted to venture down the beach for an 80 P lobster (40 Piasters to the dollar), we had to go with 2 or 3 others all armed with AR-15s. I never went for lobster, but one day I awoke on the beach with the sun over the hills *and* felt lucky the "bad guys" hadn't found me. Night life in Nha Trang consisted usually of eating at the Viet Angh Club owned by a Frenchman named Monsieur Maurice but was actually run by the Special Forces Detachment in the area. Even though Maurice knew a lot about food, the local area and people, he wasn't much of a business man, nor was his wife, who had just run Maurice's *Citroeon* car into the front pillar of the entry gate. Therefore, the local Green Beret Group took over the Club's operation by finding new sources of food supply, beef instead of water buffalo, and in some instances, even had the U S Navy bring it right to the beach right off the supply ship. Business was great, the food was outstanding, especially the French Onion Soup, but there was also an occasional night of entertainment. During one such night, a USO Troup visited the Club. Martha Raye was the star, but she was accompanied by 4 or 5 gorgeous Australian dancers. During the roof top dancing with one of the "Darwin Dolls", or whatever their name was, I wanted to try to impress one of them by turning my cigarette 180 degrees in my mouth and smoking it from the inside. I didn't make much of an impression since she danced off with a cut-in and I burned the inside of my mouth. Since Martha Raye was there, she was forever escorted by 4 or 5 Field Grade Officers since she was an Army Nurse with the rank of Lt. Col. At one point in the evening's activities, 2 or 3 of these officers were escorting Ms. (Lt. Col.) Raye outside to the next stop on their escorted tour of Nha Trang when an

RB-66 came swooping down the beach and dropped a string of about 10 photo flares as it took pictures of a suspected target. When the first ones went off with a "whoosh"-like bang, all three of Martha's escorts fell on her to protect her from a possible mortar attack. I was exiting the Club to see what was going on when I saw all three men trying to look "swave and deboner" in the act of saving her from certain doom. I think Martha had a good laugh about that. I know I did.

During our stay at Nha Trang, we were required to be inoculated with Gamma Globulin so we wouldn't contract Hepatitis during our Vietnam tour. One effect that I remember as well as all the others who were inoculated was the double shot, one in each cheek, which made it very uncomfortable returning to the Pacific Hotel and for about 6 hours afterward. Fortunately, I had ridden my bicycle to the Army Field Hospital tent and that helped me exercise my gluteus-maximus to a greater degree than those who had ridden there in a truck or Jeep.

The most popular local business in Nha Trang was the bicycle shop where one could not only buy a somewhat serviceable bicycle, but also exchange Dollars for Piasters at a varying rate of exchange, but at a better rate than the "official" rate. We could use the "P" to buy "Ba-Mui-Ba" (33 in Vietnamese), the local beer that supposedly had Formaldehyde in it, at the local bars. Unfortunately, as the Ba-Mui-Ba got us drunk, the bicycles also seemed to get tipsy and many of us fell off of them on the way home from downtown.

During the 5 ½ months at Nha Trang we had time between missions to drop ARVN Paratroops down on a drop zone named "Sandy Soil". This was good for Air Commando training, inter-service cooperation and gave the Vietnamese soldiers some extra jump-pay, so it helped everybody concerned. We were also planning to participate in the fun by being allowed to make 5 jumps apiece using ARVN equipment and our C-47s. However, before we could start the program and earn Vietnamese Jump Wings, our boss found out about the plan. In a meeting after our first drop mission, we pilots were told that, "Any of my pilots that jump out of a perfectly good airplane will be on the next one back to the States." So there went our quest for jump wings and being able to say we were jump qualified, even if not by U S standards.

One other activity kind of riled the boss and that was my reluctant decision to let a navigator make a couple of touch and go landings on a local training mission. This navigator had flown several missions with me and claimed to have flown T-28s and knew how to land a C-47, which I doubted, but I was Instructor qualified and felt I could handle anything he could throw at me. Besides, I owed him a favor due to the fact that I almost caused him to fall out of my Gooney Bird at 2500 feet out over the South China Sea. Having been an ex-Philadelphia Eagles Linebacker as well as Combat Control "Honcho", he decided to use his considerable bulk to give me some grief by moving forward and backward up and down the cargo compartment between the nav compartment and the latrine in the tail. This caused the horizontal trim to shift the nose from nose low to nose high in a matter of seconds. My counteraction was to roll the trim wheel on the left side of the throttle quadrant back and forth to adjust for the weight shift. After 2 or 3 laps back and forth, I waited until the trim needed to go nose down and instead, I pushed the nose down to achieve 0 Gravity for 3 or 4 seconds, then I jerked the yoke back to nose up. When I looked back, my Navigator, who had been floating about 2 feet off the floor, was now sitting on his "duff" right in front of the open troop door with his eyes and his mouth wide open. I think I decided never to do that again.

But now it was his turn to show me a thing or two—about how NOT to land a Gooney Bird. I had put him in the left seat as we entered the traffic pattern. I told him all the good little things he needed to know about airspeed, flap setting, gear down, Mixture Rich, Props Full Increase, all he had to do was keep the airspeed between 90 and 80 knots and aim for the runway numbers. I also warned him about what would happen if he was too fast and hit the ground nose low, or too slow and stalled before touchdown. He kept saying: "I got it—I got it—." Of course, he hit the runway too fast and bounced 10 feet in the air. He was pulling back on the yoke at 75 knots and we floated another 700 feet down the runway before we hit the second time— "I got it"—as I told him not to pull back this time. "I got it" he insisted as I added some power and attempted to hold the nose down before we stalled. After two more bounces and 5000 feet of runway, we finally managed to wrestle the bird to a standstill before I took full control and taxied in to shut down for the day. I decided not to do <u>that</u> ever again. The boss must have decided the same thing, because he almost took me off Instructor status or ground me. However, my Navigator merely picked him up by his shirt front and held him up against the wall on his tip toes and exclaimed, "Jackes is the only pilot flying the *#@&%-ing mission around here, now get off his back!"

This time, in 1965, we again were returning to home base via a Government Contract air carrier, I think this time it was ONA, Overseas National Airlines. After we left Honolulu bound for Travis AFB, one of my more resourceful Navigator buddies—"A NAVIGATOR!!"—but that's a joke that nobody can tell anymore—pulled his carry-on gym bag out from under his seat and slyly unwrapped a bottle of Chivas Regal. I had never had it before, not ever having been a Scotch drinker, but when he offered me some, I decided this was the time to try some, so I retrieved my plastic cup and put it under my tray table so Pete could pour 3 fingers. I found out right off that it really <u>was</u> the good stuff. Unfortunately, before I could do more than sample the amber elixir, a surly stewardess snuck up behind us and asked, "what is that?" When I replied, "Iced tea", she grabbed mine and sniffed it, wrinkling up her "wart-covered" nose and declared, "This is not allowed. I'm going to report you to the Captain." Then I retorted, "What's he going to do, put me out at 30,000 feet?" She grabbed both cups, marched to the rear galley and dumped out our Chivas Regal. As she strode past us to the front, I called out "I hope you get pregnant in San Francisco!"

Following our return to the "Land of the Big BX and Gold Doorknobs", as most Southeast Asians thought of the USA, the war in Vietnam was definitely heating up. Therefore, we were required to spend most of our time either on exercises or in air shows. One of our recurring Joint Operations Exercises was Cherokee Trail, which my wife, Barbara, used to call Apache Pass for some reason. During one week long stretch of playing air drop, infiltration and exfiltration—get the guerillas in, then resupply them, then air drop to the counterinsurgent force and finally, landing in a pea patch to pick up the good guys, so we had plenty of opportunities to hone our skills in the "wilds" of North Carolina. A three runway triangular ex-training base called McCall Army Airfield was our home for about 10 days. Since we flew mostly at night, we had to find some day time diversion. After rolling out of our sleeping bags, washing up in our helmets and shaving with cold water or showering in a small creek with a miniature waterfall, we went to see what was left to eat in the mess tent. One day, the army Mess Sergeant told us that if we picked enough blackberries, he would make us a big pie. So, we took our clean helmets and scurried around in the prickly underbrush, picking enough blackberries for 2 or 3 pies for us and the maintenance crews. Boy! That sure was some "good eats" as they say in Mayberry, but the cooks didn't tell us gullible flyboys that where we had found the blackberries was the most rattlesnake infested area around there. Guess they had heard us coming and didn't want to rattle or strike. Glad it wasn't the exercise Swift Strike that was held elsewhere. We also encamped for another exercise in a small town named Elerby N.C. in a Boy Scout camp. This was right after Barbara and I had married in April of 1966 and we were sent to Ft. Bragg N.C. for two weeks of Counter Insurgency Operations School run by the Army Special Warfare Center, BG Joseph Stillwell commanding. Officers from all over the World attended along with Army, Navy, Marine and Air Force personnel. At one point in the classroom training, someone had asked a question of the Army Major who was teaching us something about covert operations. When the Major told the questioner that he had already explained that point, a voice from the back of the classroom exclaimed, "Well, obviously you didn't explain it, Major, or he wouldn't have asked the question!" We all turned around to find "Vinegar Joe" Stillwell standing there, living up to his reputation.

Out in the field, on the exercise in Elerby, I had managed to secure living space at the Boy Scout camp all to myself. This seclusion afforded me the opportunity to have my new bride visit me and bring me one of my favorite dishes for a private dinner. When Barbara arrived, she was carrying my still warm dinner, a bottle of Rose wine and appropriate napery and silverware, including a candle and a wine glass. She was also accompanied by her Mother, who had somehow managed to drive her Volkswagen station wagon from Wood River in Illinois to our temporary housing outside of Ft. Bragg, NC. After sharing our Chicken and Chips Bake casserole with wife and mother-in-law, they departed and left me to finish my wine and a cigar, in near solitude—a couple of curious fellow campers wanted to know how I managed to pull that off, but I finished my wine and cigar and turned in after dismantling my "dining table"—a packing crate and a foot locker.

For one of our deployments to Cherokee Trail, I managed to bring up my MG-B from Florida that I had purchased in Saigon, right on Thu-Do Street across from the Continental Hotel. I was able to park it in a shed near our encampment so it was out of sight. It allowed two of us to go into town and seek out some sort of entertainment, completely lacking at our operations camp site that was our Blue Force HQ. The first time we returned from one of our "recon" sorties, I was walking into the Operations tent and our Commander handed me a canteen cup with a clear liquid in it. After the first sip, I stopped in mid-stride and croaked, "J---- C-----! What the Hell IS this?" His reply was, "That's South Carolina Moonshine, Boy." He and another officer had been to town also, and had met the Deputy County Sheriff at a diner and had asked him where they could find some local "spirits". They were led to his patrol car, and there in the trunk was a supply of local "hooch". He was told it was the best in the County—that he only confiscated the good stuff. I had never had any before, but it was pure and powerful as far as I could tell. It was supposedly 180-proof, or 90% alcohol. We even had to mix it with Pepsi Cola to stomach it.

I had really enjoyed my MG-B except for three things. On most summer days in Ft. Walton Beach it was too hot to have the top down and when the top was down in the evening, sometime around 1 AM, I would be awakened in my beach house by the rumble of thunder as the Crestview Monsoon would sneak down to the beach and lay a downpour on us unsuspecting rag-top owners. At that point, I would have to slosh out to my topless MG-B, under the dripping Spanish Moss, and wrestle the rails and leather top from the trunk and assemble the frame in the support brackets, pull them apart, stretch the top over them and try to snap it in place while shivering in my shorts. About the third time in a month of that routine, I decided to get rid of the car and buy something cooler with a solid top.

I found a car dealer in Ft. Walton Beach who had had

previous sales experience with Plymouths. Since I had decided that I had to have a Plymouth *Barracuda*, 1964, with a 273 cu. In. engine and a 4-speed Hurst floor shift. I ordered one from Glen, who assured me that he could find one to be delivered to his car lot in about a month or so. In the meantime, I had acquired a '53 Mercury 4-door in which to drive around while I waited for my powerful Plymouth.

When I returned from Dominican Republic, there were three messages for me that my new car was in and had been for about two weeks. So I dragged my Merc with the cracked block so I could get rid of it and start enjoying my new "dragster". Glen had given me such a great trade in on my MG-B, almost as much as I had paid for it in Saigon, I could easily afford to trade up to the "Cuda". When he handed me the keys, I jumped in and cranked it up. Just as I did, Glen was walking behind it and almost jumped across Eglin Parkway when the big square tailpipe roared with a VAROOM! He asked me, "What the Hell was THAT!" I told him, "THAT'S a 'Ba-Ra-Cocka-Duda, Baby!" He took a long look and listen as I revved it up a couple of times. When I shut down in order to go inside and sign the papers, he looked back and said, "I still think you screwed me on this deal."

It wasn't long before another co-pilot in the Squadron had bought his '64 Mustang with a 289 V-8 and the first time we met on the Eglin Parkway, when it was a lot less congested than now, we decided automatically to find out which was faster. Well, he won, but when I decided to accept defeat rather than press our luck, I turned left toward town while he continued around the dual-lane parkway to the west, where he was stopped for speeding.

During a day-night navigation training mission out over the Gulf of Mexico, I had the opportunity to be flying "Puff the Magic Dragon"—our camouflaged C-47 with three 7.62mm Gatling Guns in the last three windows of the left side. Even though we weren't carrying any ammunition, we looked like the legendary gun bird. After our navigation leg of 2 hours out south and 2 hours back north so the Navigators could train in celestial navigation at night over water, we ended up going into Moissant International to drop off the Lt. Col Instructor Navigator so he could go on leave. It was about 9 or 10 at night, during the Air Traffic Controllers strike, and without any other air traffic in the area we landed to the south and went right to the Terminal to drop off our passenger. We swung around to let him out the troop door and didn't even have to shut down an engine. As we sat there waiting, the Tower Controller asked, "Are those things loaded?" It hadn't even dawned on me that the three guns were pointing directly at the Terminal (As Johnny Carson, as Aunt Blabby, would say, "Don't say Terminal to an old person!") I assured him that we weren't carrying any ammunition. For takeoff, we were cleared right back to the same runway on which we had landed to the south and made our quick departure to the north. I think they were glad to get rid of us.

Our blissful life in Louisiana was punctuated by some fond and not so fond experiences, involving a swimming pool, a gay, color-blind florist, a T-34 buzz-job, a Cardinal football game and another trip to New Orleans.

The swimming pool at our apartment complex—not very complex with only about 15 units in only two stories— was the social focus of the 25 or 30 residents. In the summertime, it was so warm in the summer sun that, as Red Skelton quipped, "I should have brought along some TIDE and rinsed out a few things." However, during the rest of the year, especially on weekends, there was always a die-hard group of pool people with various degrees of garb, to create a party atmosphere. We all shared the duty of mixing Margaritas, blending a can of frozen limeade with a cup of Tequila and a tray of ice cubes in our blenders for all to share. As the frozen limeade was thawing, the ice cubes were re-freezing and the music was playing from the speakers of whomever had the closest and the loudest stereo, or I guess it was only hi-fi then, in their window, not to mention something always on the grill, another shared responsibility, be it hot dogs, hamburgers, bratwurst, or the upstairs gay guy's favorite, dirty rice. The only thing my Mother-in-Law and I agreed on, besides her Daughter, was that we both wanted a houseboat, but on one occasion of her visit to "Coon-Ass Country", we went to a local lake for her to go fishing. After several beers and not any success at the fishin' hole, we purchased a watermelon from a local produce vendor on the way home. Since the melon was way bigger than our meager refrigerator, I did what I thought was expedient, and tossed the watermelon into our pool. After it bottomed out, it bobbled around for the rest of the night and was relatively cool in the morning for our next poolside get-together.

One of the gay guys, who fixed the dirty rice, was named Jerry and he was a florist. He was also color-blind, so we asked him the obvious question. He said that he couldn't see in color, but recognized various shades of gray as either red, blue, green or shades in between. It worked for him, but would have kept me out of the Air Force. One weekend, the St. Louis Football Cardinals were playing a pre-season game up in Monroe, La. (pronounced: <u>Mon-row</u>), and my sports-enthusiast bride wanted to go so she could see our new Quarterback, Jim Hart in his first season as a Cardinal. I had to gallivant off to North Carolina or wherever, so Jerry offered to escort her to Monroe to see the game. I felt secure in acceding to that offer. During the '67-'68 season, we actually were able to see Jim Hart play in Busch Stadium in St. Louis.

On one of those occasions, I checked out the Aero Club's T-34 for a cross-country trip from Alexandria, La. to the airport in Bethalto IL, so we could visit in Wood River and go to St. Louis to see a football game. The flight would take a little over 4 hours, so I planned to make a refueling stop at the place where I had learned to fly the T-34, Malden, Mo. Upon arrival there, I found the local fuel agent—I swear he had a hayseed in his mouth—and asked him to refuel our T-34, while I explained not only the virtues of the airplane, but also how I had arrived there. Since the Air Force wasn't paying for my gas, I quickly checked my pocket and checked how much I could afford to put in the tanks. Seven and a half dollars was the total, and even at 1967 gas prices, that wasn't going to put much "go-water" in the tanks. However, I felt it was enough for the rest of the trip added to what meager fuel I had landed with so, on to Bethalto. If my wife had been a better navigator, we wouldn't have wasted time almost landing at Walnut Ridge, Arkansas, before I found out it wasn't our destination. In her defense, both airfields were laid out in the same triangular pattern and were on almost the same heading from Louisiana and only about 60 miles apart on our navigation chart. Anyway, upon arrival at Bethalto, before it was St. Louis Regional Airport, I requested a 360° degree overhead pattern, a-la pilot training and fighter pattern, and lined up on initial for an unusual arrival that should (like at Webb AFB?) excite the relatives watching us from the ramp. As soon as I rolled crisply to the left, the engine quit as if I'd shut off the mag switch. Remembering my almost forgotten Emergency Procedures, I quickly reached down, turned on the Boost Pump Switch and changed the Fuel Tank Selector to the left tank. That did the trick, the engine restarted and we landed smoothly as if nothing had happened at all. Of course, her mother almost had a heart attack, but I assured her that that happened all the time when the fuel level was low in the down-wing tank and there was nothing wrong with the airplane. When I inquired about refueling, I was advised that I had only about ½ a gallon left. Needless to say, I found a way to pay for a full load of fuel for the trip home. The return trip was a little less exciting, but it did have its high points. Since the weather was supposed to be relatively clear with no rain or showers, I filed VFR (Visual Flight Rules) all the way to Alexandria. There was supposed to be a little cloud cover for the first part of the trip, but clearing as we flew through Arkansas and into Louisiana. It was a beautiful day for takeoff and climb to 4500 feet—even plus 500 feet westbound for VFR—and we had no trouble following the "Big Muddy" south to the Ozarks, but, as the terrain rose, the cloud deck, as well as the visibility, came down forcing our little T-34 down to 2500 feet. As we dodged hill tops in low visibility, we began to pick up radio calls from Pine Bluff Flight Following. We were to contact Pine Bluff Radio, which at that time and position and altitude, we were unable to do. At this point, I decided to land there and refuel, just in case, about 30 minutes further on. We landed in now pretty good weather and terrain and taxied to the ramp. As Barbara supervised the refueling, since she had the money from her mother to be sure we didn't run out this time, I went in to find out what all the radio calls had been about and why Air Traffic Control had been so anxious to hear from us. I was told that they just wanted to know if they should close out our Flight Plan. Therefore, I filed a Continuation Flight Plan for the final leg of our trip to Alexandria. The rest of the trip home was very pleasant, with clear skies and light winds. I could see England AFB 20 miles out and nobody was looking for us since we would have our trusty bird back in the Aero Club before dark and we closed out our Flight Plan with the tower upon landing.

Following one of the exercises in North Carolina and a final night of "celebrating" with some Green Berets, we loaded up our Gooney Bird and headed home to Louisiana. As we approached Atlanta, I was trying to stay awake in the right seat when I looked to the left to see my co-pilot nodding off also. I decided that, since he was in the left seat and was going to make the landing, it would be best for him to snooze a bit, so I said, "One of us has to stay awake, so you go ahead and sleep and I'll wake you before we get there." It was a beautiful clear day and it was entertaining to scan the Mississippi River noting how the bends and twists discerned where the river bed had moved here and there over hundreds of years. About 100 miles out of England AFB, I requested a VFR letdown at pilot's discretion and started a 100-200 feet per minute rate of descent. Evidently, I had timed it just right because I had the runway in sight at 900 feet about 1 ½ miles out on a base leg. I lowered the landing gear, put the flaps to 1/4 inside 1 mile on final, called the tower and received clearance to land. At this point, I woke up my dozing co-pilot, saying, "You got it!" After realizing where he was with the runway right in front of him, he tried to do everything to put the airplane in landing configuration. I told him, "Just land it!" He bounced only once, then said, "J---- C-----! Everybody ought to try that just once." The adrenalin was really rushing. I told him, "That's the last time you'll go to sleep with me on the airplane."

One of my stunts of which I am least proud was the day I had had a few drinks and decided to go out to the Aero Club and take the T-34 up for a joy-ride. In my "enlightened" condition I went over Alexandria and found our apartment building. After one low pass to see if anybody was around to watch, I climbed to 2000 feet and proceeded to dive down toward the swimming pool and zoomed over the roof at 100 feet or less. It got everybody's attention at the apartment. Fortunately, nobody called the Base and reported me.

One of my other co-pilots fancied himself as the "World's greatest Gooney Bird Pilot". One day, at England AFB, he had a chance to prove it. We were flying a local training mission featuring short field landings and take offs. We began a contest with my demonstrating a minimum distance take off followed by a minimum distance landing from the right seat, which was backward for me, as I was so used to the left seat and the throttles in my right hand and a left seat perspective. After one such demonstration, I turned the practice over to John Rauch, my fellow racing partner from Ft. Walton Beach in 1964 between his '64 Mustang and my "64 Barracuda, which he won handily—289 vs. 273 cu. in. even with my 4-speed Hurst Shifter. Now it was time for revenge, so I challenged my racing foe to a short-field landing contest. My first was between the 9000 and the 8000 feet remaining markers, not very good for a true Air Commando expert. His first was about a hundred feet shorter, my next was at about 800 feet—on and on to abuse the old C-47, until we finally quit with his score about 690 feet vs. 700 feet for me. I "picked up my chips" and vowed revenge at a later date to redeem my rightful title as "World's Greatest Gooney Bird Pilot".

During my flying career, I was required to attend several survival schools, one of which was Tactical Air Command's Deep Sea Survival—40 hours of fun in the sun and waters of Biscayne Bay out of Homestead AFB FL. After learning how to extricate oneself from the pilot's seat after plunging down a slide into a swimming pool, we had to haul ourselves out of the water and into a one-man raft or a 6-man raft to begin the survival phase of the course. We learned how to find survival items such as signal flares, a mirror, whistle, canned water, fishing gear, rations and a de-Salinization still, which we would learn to use once we were sent out into Biscayne Bay. Our final test was to practice our newly-learned skills while actually floating away from shore in a one-man raft. Some pilots, mainly single engine ones, had the thrill of being allowed to parasail off of a platform behind a power boat to be dropped into the water after their simulated parachute fall and then maneuvering themselves into their life raft. I wanted to do that, but, since I was a multi-engine type, I didn't get to participate in that phase of training. I managed to find the fishing kit and simple lures. I attached the hook, lure and leader to the nylon fishing line and un-reeled it out to about 20-30 feet. I was contemplating the odds of ever catching anything when there was a sudden jerk on the line and then a strong pull, so strong that the little raft and I started following with the thin fishing line about to cut off my finger that was holding it. At that point, I found my survival knife and quickly cut the line. Whatever I had cut loose obviously wanted that lure more than I wanted it. I later figured out that I had probably hooked a Manta Ray— not on the list of approval for survival supplement.

There are several places in the U.S. that I don't think I ever want to see again. One of them is Watertown, N.Y. It has to be one of the most environmentally inhospitable places in the Northern Hemisphere, of course I only saw it in the middle of Winter. We, (since I was flying a transport with 2 or 3 crewmembers), were scheduled to drop a few Army paratroopers up in the Ft. Drum area in Western New York. We were coming north from Florida and North Carolina with our intrepid Ft. Bragg paratroopers when we received our destination weather report—so cold that the ground was frozen, snow covered and unusable as a drop zone. Therefore, we were to land at the radar site at Watertown, drop off our Army troops, spend the night at the radar site, and, weather permitting, return the next day. The folks at the radar site were very hospitable with food, booze and movies since there wasn't much else for entertainment in the local, snow-covered area in below zero chill factor. So, after a congenial night and a good sleep, it was time to crank up our trusty Gooney Birds and "di-di-mao", or get the Hell out of there, to return to the warmth of Florida. There were two crews of us up there and each of us was anxious to get back home. My crew and I tried and tried to start both engines, but with almost zero fuel pressure on NO. 1 engine after starting NO. 2, we just couldn't get NO. 1 started. Before I burned out the starter on the left engine, we decided to call it quits and ask for help in hopes that we could be airborne before it got even colder and the snow got deeper. As we were working out a solution to our no-start problem, the other crew taxied past us on its way to take off position while the A/C thumbed his nose at me. They made it off, while we watched, enviously, still trying to find a way to follow them home. About a frigid and unfruitful hour later, we shut down our attempts to attain fuel pressure and went inside to thaw out and called home to the Command Post for a solution. The solution was to bring Herman Nelson Heaters from Griffiss AFB to heat the R-1830s so we could operate normally and start both engines. When that solution was successful, I left the crew on board so I could call back home and report our progress as well as thank our saviors personally. At the end of our conversation, the Command Post advised me, "Oh, by the way, you'll need to stop in Syracuse so you can pick up Dave Wroblewski and his crew—they lost an engine an hour out of Watertown". That made up for the nose-thumbing earlier, but guess who had to return a few days later to test hop the new engine and return a cold Gooney Bird to the warm haven of Hurlburt Fld., FL? Before leaving Watertown, I received another call requesting that I take a slight detour to Glenn's Falls NY to drop off a Lt. Col from the Special Warfare Center so he could attend his wife's funeral. Since it was only 135 miles through the beautiful, snow-covered Adirondack Mountains, I filed a VFR Flight Plan direct to Glenn's Falls, dropped down to the Warren County Airport and left our very grateful passenger on the snowy ramp with a wave and a salute. Then it was back to warm and sunny Florida, glad to be out of New York in winter. I received a nice thank you letter of commendation from the Special Warfare Center and I still have the US Army field jacket that was the only item I requested in return.

One of the most memorable stories related during my classroom training in the Counterinsurgency Operations Officer Course at the Special Warfare Center was that of a North Vietnamese family, obviously dedicated to the cause of the Viet Cong, who were tasked with transporting three 75mm artillery shells from their home in the north to a certain Viet Cong Major conducting warfare against the "Imperialists" down in the Delta region of South Vietnam. After three months of trekking through mountains, mud, rain storms and even B-52 bombardments, this lowly "mule" and his wife, who were carrying these three 75mm shells, finally found their recipient and turned over their carefully concealed cargo. Without any display of gratitude, the Major told the weary man, "Very good, now go back and bring me three more." This was a tale designed to teach us just what kind of enemy we were fighting. It made a great impression on me for a long time.

During my Air Commando training a Hurlburt Fld., Fla., in a conversation with Joe Holden, an intrepid T-28 pilot, he advised me that, if I ever had a chance to be assigned to Taiwan, I should definitely take it—that it was the best kept secret in the United States Air Force.

Four years later, Barbara and I received orders reassigning us from England AFB to the Military Assistance Institute in Arlington Va. Having no idea of just what MAI was or who B/G Royal Reynolds who had signed the welcome letter, was, I queried my friend and fellow Gooney Bird pilot in Personnel. He reluctantly told me that he wasn't allowed to divulge my future destination because Tactical Air Command hadn't released my yet. I thought it was because I was such a valuable C-47 pilot that TAC didn't want me to go elsewhere. However, a few days later, my Personnel friend informed me that MAI was like a charm school for diplomats assigned overseas as part of Military Assistance Advisory Group (MAAG), just like those in Vietnam under the command of General William Westmoreland, but this was Taipei, Taiwan, not Saigon Vietnam.

CHAPTER 11

HOW DO YOU SAY THAT IN CHINESE

Our drive from Alexandria LA to Arlington VA took us by way of Myrtle Beach NC where we decided to stay for a day and night before reporting in to Royal Reynold's "Charm School. It was late March and we chose to venture out to the beach to enjoy the sun and sand even if it wasn't the "season" as yet on the Atlantic Strand. As the temperature struggled to reach 77 degrees, we crouched behind a canvas shelter to hide from the wind and didn't dare go in the surf, but we did "hit the beach", the last time for the next two years.

While residing at the Arlington Towers, with our miniature apartment on the 7th floor and the school in the Basement, we settled into an academic routine near Washington DC with nothing for Barbara to do but hang around with the other wives and sightsee around the nation's capital.

Since we were being assigned to Taiwan, even though we weren't going to learn Chinese, we were introduced to Chinese Culture. We even had one Army Major who was to be assigned to the Chief of Police in Taipei who could speak and write Chinese, but his Oriental-looking wife couldn't speak or read Chinese. Our introduction to the Chinese mind set came by way of a dinner at the O Mai Restaurant in Washington DC. We were seated in groups of 2 or 4 or 6 around the table with an equal number of our Chinese hosts, both civilian and military. This taught us that tables of more than 2 always seated an even number of people because odd numbers are unlucky. Our second lesson was the habit of toasting one's guests with tea or an alcoholic beverage with a rousing "Gam-Bei!" as everyone downed his glass which was immediately refilled in preparation for the next toast. It is considered bad form (loss of face) to overdo the Gam Beis and need assistance to leave the table. One particular General in Taiwan had one too many toasts and had to be helped from the party by his aide. He was never seen socially in public again. I think the Chinese hosts were testing me the same way. Another insight into the Chinese Culture was when the man next to me noticed my facility with chop sticks and remarked, "Oh, Captain, you use chopsticks very well." I responded that I had learned at the Pearl City Tavern, or PCT, near Pearl Harbor in Honolulu and enjoyed using them when I had the opportunity. Then he asked me if I could pick up a pea off my dinner plate with chopsticks. After I accomplished that little feat, he said, "Very good, Captain. Now, can you pick up two peas?" Of course it wasn't easy, but I managed to capture 2 peas and get them in my mouth without dropping them, which brought an immediate "Gam Bei!".

While I was attending Military Assistance Institute, Barbara and I had many opportunities to visit the Officer's Club at Ft. Meyer, VA, which was a great place to hob-nob with other officers of every rank and service and even nationalities. The Happy Hours were always fun as well as educational. There were always lively discussions about current events and/or politics, even occasionally flying and of course, the war in Vietnam, which covered all three subjects. I found ears for many of my flying experiences for almost 5 years of being an Air Commando. Following one such entertaining evening after more than a few drinks for each of us, Barbara was "resting" in front of the TV wearing nothing but a black lace slip which had ridden up her bare legs as high as they went. The sight of that "Sleeping Beauty" got me so excited that, face down and sleeping or not, I couldn't resist the urge. Nine months later, in Taiwan, our son, Burris, was born.

But before we had to report to Military Assistance Institute, we had only a short time to ship our household goods to Taiwan to await our arrival some 4 or 5 weeks later. We also needed to ship our four year old Volkswagen out of New Orleans for our inexpensive transportation for our two years of driving around the Island of Taiwan and city of Taipei. We had no idea what that would be like, but since it was Barbara's car, we felt she could handle the local traffic in it. We, therefore, headed South again from Alexandria to re-visit New Orleans, her in the VW and me following in my *Barracuda*, in which we would travel back to Alexandria, on to Arlington VA and eventually to Seattle WA for our long flight to Taipei. Once we arrived in the "Big Easy", we first took care of the car shipment, hopefully accompanying our household goods through the Panama Canal, so they would arrive together. However, we found out that the car would arrive first so that we would have transportation to Keelung to pick up our household goods when they arrived a bit later. We would also need it to look around the area for suitable housing in which to put them. With this unsettling knowledge about our first Permanent Change of Station (PCS), we decided to spend a day or two calming our apprehension by hitting some of the high spots in New Orleans. The weather in March was cold, windy and rainy. We seemed to have entered the Bourbon Street "marathon"—running as fast as we could from bar to bar in horizontal rain at 50-54 degrees temperature. I remember starting out at the Circus Lounge, a revolving bar on the first floor of the Monte Leone Hotel where we were staying. We drank a local bar favorite, a Sazarak, or Mint Julep or something, maybe my old favorite, Old Fashion. We had a good running start up one side and down the other of Bourbon Street. We eventually ended up at T. Pitarri's, a well-known restaurant that served wild game of elk, pheasant and bear. I don't remember what all I consumed, but I did receive a gourmet certificate signed by the owner for my gastronomic adventure and taste. When we returned to Alexandria to arrange for shipment of our household goods, we had a little "clean out the refrigerator and liquor cabinet" party and I was able to show off my Gourmet Certificate to our guests, some of whom were suitably impressed since I had already been written up in the Base Newspaper as a local wine connoisseur, even if I did occasionally resort to Boone's Farm for bar-be-ques.

Now it was time to leave "Coon-ass Country" and drive to Seattle for our trip to our new home. My best friend from high school and college lived, and still does, in Camarillo Calif., so we stopped there for a day before venturing up the Coastal Highway through Monterey and Carmel before continuing up the center of California to Victoria in Washington, just across the Columbia River from Portland Oregon. We had a beautiful water-side dinner and a really good night's sleep and then pressed on to our motel right near Fairchild AFB and Seattle-Tacoma International Airport. Our only problem now was where to sell our beloved *Barracuda* before boarding the 747 in two days. I tried one used car lot after another, of which there were many as around any large military base, especially any near a coastal departure airport. I finally had to settle on the one buyer who said, "Captain, what's the best offer you've had so far?" I had to admit that my best offer had been $1000. He said he'd give me $1050 just to get the car that he liked and knew it would sell easily but he told me it needed a new paint job, tires and 2nd synchro was going. I was tired of the runaround, so I took his offer and returned to the motel knowing that I had had to deal with a buyer's market and $1050 was probably the best I could do. On the way to the airplane the next day, we passed right by the used car lot and there was my beautiful shiny Barracuda right out in front with a neon yellow price tag on the windshield of $1995. I'll bet he had that $945 profit in his pocket before we landed in Taiwan.

Once we arrived in Taiwan, we had a lot to learn, not only about a foreign country, but about earthquakes, New Taiwan Dollars, language and domestic help. First, we had to meet our sponsors, who turned out to be Herb and Marie Dagg, a delightful couple who would become good friends. They and the Galloways, who were our boss and wife and who had been there the longest time, took us from the airport to the hotel in downtown Taipei. There, we learned first-hand about the seismic phenomenon of at least one earthquake a day. In fact, the first night there, we felt the floor shake and one of the pictures on the hotel room wall went "slonchwise". We were assured that there was nothing to worry about and to just have another drink, also an introduction into Taiwan social life.

I soon found out why Joe Holden had considered Taiwan such a plum assignment. Not only was the cost of living as low as we could imagine, we found very little language problem; the Taiwanese were very friendly and most all spoke English, which was good because learning Chinese was even harder than Vietnamese even though it, too, was a tonal language. The biggest problem, as my wife and father-in-law found out, is that there are three separate dialects—Mandarin, Cantonese and Taiwanese. When Barbara was trying to learn the language, she found out that, while she was trying to learn Mandarin, one person would be speaking Cantonese and our Amah spoke Taiwanese so she couldn't even practice at home. One incident confirmed the difficulty of the different dialects. When my father-in-law was watching people and traffic come and go on the busy thoroughfare in front of his downtown hotel in 1968, he witnessed one of our officer's wife get rear-ended right in front of him by one of the 88,000 taxicabs in Taipei. As the hotel doorman, the taxi driver and his passenger and our friend, who spoke a little

Chinese, were shouting at each other, no one could understand the other as one was speaking Mandarin, the doorman was speaking Cantonese and the taxi driver was only fluent in Taiwanese. The traffic cop was only standing there observing, which is all Taipei traffic policemen ever did. The whole time, my father-in-law was rolling his movie camera and recording it all.

Our Amah (Chinese nursemaid) was a God-send. We inherited her from the people we replaced and she was happy to leave their employ for a couple of reasons. Harry was short-tempered which occasionally manifested itself in fits of crude behavior. The main reason, of course, was the fact that Barbara was pregnant and Sheesa loved being able to take care of babies. We were glad to have her.

One sidelight I found out later about my predecessor was an incident that occurred during a routine flight to Kadena AFB in Okinawa. One of my passengers told me the story about how Harry had come back to ask this Contractor if he had ever been to Okinawa before. When he answered "yes", Harry asked him what it looked like. They had been in the air for 2 hours heading east, and still hadn't seen the island. The Contractor then said, "We're lost, aren't we, Harry." After turning around and tuning in a Kadena NAVAID, they finally arrived at destination. I don't know how Harry could have missed the island completely, but that was Harry.

Our little "Up hillside village" house was a God-send also. We only paid 3000 NT a month, about $75, for a two bedroom house with a garage and a maid's room off the kitchen. Sheesa was there 5 ½ days and nights a week, did all the cleaning and cooking for only $30 a month. After a year, I tried to raise her to $35 a month, and was accused of trying to ruin the economy. We also had a houseboy named Liao who pedaled his bicycle up the hill on Sunday to stoke the water heater with coal, polish the brass and wax the teakwood furniture as well as the parquet floors, all for $5 a weekend. On the Sunday that he did the floors, he would bring his own electric buffer perched on the back of his bike. He also helped with the fireplace in the living room by relining the brick with aluminum foil so the heat of the fire would reflect back into the house. Since the weather in Taipei was a lot like that in New Orleans, the temperature could drop to 50-55 in the winter, the fireplace was used many times, especially with a baby to keep warm. In order to keep the bedroom warm however, we had to purchase a reverse-cycle air conditioner through the Navy Exchange and it worked just fine, cooling in the summer and heating in the winter. We also had a kerosene heater that I had brought back from Hong Kong that radiated heat to anyone sitting near it. When my wife called me on a cool day in November about a month before Burris's first birthday, she told me he had uttered his first word. I didn't have to ask what it was, as active as he was I knew it had to be "HOT!" It didn't surprise me at all.

Since we were located in the "middle" Far East, I was witness to much traffic outside my office window as aircrews and personnel were traveling between Okinawa, Japan, Philippines, Hong Kong and Vietnam. It was said, that if you stayed there long enough, you would see everybody you ever knew in the Air Force. The U S Flight Ops office was located in the Chinese Air Force (CAF) terminal area adjacent to the VIP lounge and next to the Passenger Information Center (PIC), of which I was in charge. This meant that when I wasn't flying up and down the Island or off to Kadena, Clark or Hong Kong, I was taking care of Admin, Scheduling, Budget as well as the PIC, and was able to see all the passengers coming and going from all directions. It was also the unofficial "Far-Eastern Furniture Trans-shipment Center" of the World as I named it. I saw many pedi-cabs, stereo cabinets, bars and papa-san chairs flowing through the door to waiting aircraft as well as ceramic elephants from Vietnam (where do you think I got mine?)

One of those "exotic" ports of call was the US of A. The Generalissimo, Chiang Kai Shek, had a beautiful, shiny C-118 for his own transportation, as well as for whomever he wanted to use it. That included the Taiwan Little League team of 1968. I wasn't there when the team loaded up its gear and boarded the shiny, luxurious DC-6B bound for the U S, but I was there 2 or 3 weeks later when a jubilant group of victorious teen-age boys deplaned in front of our office to great cheers of mothers, fathers and many well-wishers. It was like a holiday the way everybody in Taiwan was celebrating the Little League World Series win, similar to what it would be like if the Cubs won the World Series in Chicago.

The last time I saw that shiny airplane in front of my window, without having to have the shades drawn, was after it had been flown back, again from the United States, following its periodic IRAN, Inspect and Replace- As-Necessary, possibly at McClellan AFB. The crew and certain VIPs, plus some friends of the "G-Mo", all had stayed in the "Land of the Big BX" for the duration of the aircraft maintenance period sight-seeing and buying all sorts of items on their "to-buy" list. When that new, even shinier C-118 taxied up to our window, it became a warehouse to be unloaded by an army of those who had ordered all those items to be brought back from the U S. I witnessed band instruments by the dozen as well as crate after crate of oranges and grapefruit. It took about 45 minutes to unload it all.

The weather in the Far East was typically tropical with its share of and what most careful pilots wouldn't want to fly through, similar to the southeast of the U S. While I was there for 2 years, I witnessed three typhoons. The first was Typhoon Shirley that blew through Hong Kong. We knew it was coming, but not before we were to arrive, so we pressed on, hoping not to bounce around the passengers too severely. From the time we left the Island and proceeded out over water, the turbulence became more pronounced, to the extent that I thought I'd better go back to the cabin and see if anybody was feeling ill, and reassure the 21 passengers, including my wife, that the good ol' Gooney Bird would make it in for a safe landing. That was a green-looking bunch as I swayed on the overhead jump cable and surveyed them. I found out after we had landed as advertised that my wife was the only one who didn't get sick. Now, the only unknown was where the Typhoon would come ashore. For sure, it was going to call for an extra day and night in Hong Kong, not a bad thing, but how much shopping would we be able to do? We had a little time to hit the usual places, but as the wind picked up and the rain started, we migrated closer and closer to our hotel. The bar and dining room were on the 6th (top) floor and all the windows were boarded up. We could feel the whole hotel shaking as the storm hit with full force. After about an hour and a half, the wind and rain decreased to practically nothing as the eye of Typhoon Shirley came right up Nanking East Road and everything seemed normal again. I received a call that it was time to go out to Kai Tak International and tend to our "Douglas Racer" before the eye passed and the storm hit again. My Flight Mechanic knew that even stronger winds were coming from a different direction, so I climbed up the 17° degree slope of the slick floor in wet shoes to the cockpit so I could release the brakes and unlock the tail wheel so a few Air China "coolies" could turn the airplane 90° degrees so it would still be into the wind, then tied down with three concrete-filled oil drums. Then we sloshed back to our hotel taxi and returned to shelter. As we were heading back, we noticed tree limbs and store signs down in the street. Power was out in most of the Kowloon side of Hong Kong, but we found a local bar on the same street as our hotel and stopped in for a beer or two. The old Chinese lady who owned the bar had on a yellow slicker and had a lantern on the bar for illumination. As we drank our beer by lamplight, three Canadian sailors came in from the increasing wind and rain looking for some more "R&R" fun. The Chinese lady laughed at their disheveled appearance and raised her lantern and said, "Ha, Ha, typhoon come in—look what come out!"

Of course, the favorite destination of anyone flying in the Far East was Hong Kong. There, one could find almost anything to buy, rather cheaply, that one could imagine from clothing to artifacts, to stereo equipment and furniture. Since we could have beautiful teakwood furniture made in Taiwan and it was difficult to bring back on the airplane, most of the affluent military officers with whom I associated were very "into" stereo equipment and clothing. On my initial checkout flight to Hong Kong I was introduced to the Manager of the hotel at which all the Air Force aircrews and passengers stayed. I was also led down the street to the House of Vashi. Most of the R&R-ers from Taiwan went to see Mr. Vashi as soon as they had checked in the hotel and refreshed a bit. As soon as the Aircraft Commander entered the shop from the street, if Mr. Vashi were in the front, he would ask, "Yes, Captain (or Major), how many people you bring me today—what you want to drink?" The Indians owned most of the tailoring business in Hong Kong and had the capacity to fabricate pants, shirts, jackets, suits within 24 hours or less. Your measurements were taken at the first meeting and after that, you came by 4 or 5 hours later for the fitting and final adjustments and by 7 or 8 in the evening, your goods would be delivered to your room at the hotel. If you wanted a couple of suits or coats made, you might have to wait until the next day's airplane to return to Taiwan with your package. You paid your account by credit card. I had my own account with Mr. Vashi, but I ordered something that took more than a day to produce, I think it was a brocade dinner jacket. I had given my tailor my "business card" which depicted the Paladin chess figure of a knight with a pot belly and a cigarette that read: "Have Goon—Will Travel—wire Jackes, Taipei." One day, a package arrived in Ops from Mr. Vashi and it was addressed to "Wire Jackes, Taipei." Well, it got there anyway—just like the green ceramic elephants which our Supply Officer had acquired by my request in Saigon and had them shipped via Chinese LST to Keelung and eventually to my office with only masking tape on top with my address in my name. Hal Ball was a very good Supply Officer, and ingenious, too.

Everybody had to have ceramic elephants from Vietnam, but also everyone had to have stereo equipment—the latest and greatest. Half my missions to Hong Kong were for trips to the Fleet Store to buy either, new stereo equipment, turn tables, amps, speakers etc., or to exchange the outdated sets for the newest and best in fashion. I stayed with Fischer for mine, but it was TEAC one month, JBL the next, then Kenwood...on and on. One of our Bridge-playing couples had 28 speakers in their living room and when we were playing Bridge at their house, the host, an Army Major/Artillery, would put on the 1812 Overture, and when the cannons roared toward the end, I swear you could hear the cannon balls going from one end of the room to the other. Since all military personnel on Taiwan only had 2 R&R trips a year, I always had a few lists for trips to the Fleet Store and may even have brought some of those speakers to Taipei, although they would have been more suited to the VC-54. That bird was fitted with a red-flocked wall paper suite and I once saw the whole aisle to the front filled with ceramic elephants. It would have been hard to secure that many on the sloping floor of my C-47.

Hong Kong was like the San Francisco of the Orient and even more exhilarating than Bangkok in 1963. During my 2 years of flying from Taipei, I made several trips to Kadena AFB on Okinawa. It was only a little over 100 miles from Taipei and had many attractive diversions, a fine Officer's Club as well as those of the Army, Navy and

Marines. It also had a good number of DoD school teachers who frequented these clubs on a nightly rotating basis, depending on what the special menus, drinks or entertainment was being furnished. If one knew the social schedule of these nightly events, one could easily find some female companionship.

One such scheduled event was Mongolian Bar-B-Q. I was first introduced to it in Taipei at a local restaurant right near our house. Somebody had told me not to eat in a store without a front on it, but on a Saturday afternoon, I would go down the hill a ways and have a haircut, shave and massage for 30NT, or about 80 cents US, then go sit inside this local eatery that didn't have a front, but did have a large wood-fired grill on the sidewalk. For about $1.25, one could purchase a large bowl of meat and vegetables with sauces and seasonings hand- picked and placed (heaped) in the bowl, then taken out to the sidewalk grill master to do his mastery with 2' chopsticks while mixing and turning the whole olio on the grill to perfection, back into the bowl, a fresh one, piping hot with a cleaning sweep of his tongs. This was accompanied by a large sesame seed roll which was hollowed out to be stuffed with the meat and vegetable mixture and washed down with a quart of Taiwan Beer. Since it was so popular in Taipei at our O. Club once a month and since the biggest and best BBQ grills were fabricated in Taipei, the O. Club at Kadena decided to add Mongolian BBQ to its monthly calendar. However, they didn't have a grill, so when one was built for the club, I was tasked with assuring that it was transported to Kadena. When it was delivered to Sung Shan International/CAF AB, I had arranged for a C-97 from Guam to add the grill to its cargo destined for Okinawa. It took 6 "coolies" to carry that cast iron grill, about 3' around, made of welded strips, out to the waiting C-97, a large, double-decked, four engine cargo plane. When the Loadmaster began to winch the grill up into the rear cargo bay by a chain pulley, the C-97 almost tipped back on its tail. By shifting some heavy cargo forward (maybe furniture), he was able to winch the grill aboard and stow it closer to the center of gravity. After the Kadena Club had its new grill, the Club Officer offered me free Mongolian BBQ any time I was there when it was on the menu. Unfortunately, I never made it back before my tour ended. The last time I was there, I had Barbara with me, but we had been on a short R&R, so we didn't have our own airplane with us in which to return to Taipei because we had hitched a ride on the swanky VC-54. Therefore, we had to call the Airlift Section to arrange for airlift back to Taiwan. We had to leave Kadena ASAP because the Base was under siege by the local Islanders who were demanding that the Island of Okinawa be returned to Japanese rule and control. In other words: "Yankee, go home!" Fortunately, most of the local workers had been "trapped" on Base when the gates were secured and the U S Military had maintained control of all the facilities. It seemed that the local workers, mostly maids and waitresses, were content to stay where they were, safe from the unruly protesters and secure where they were still being paid to work. Finally, our comrades-in-arms came and rescued us, returning us home and ending our adventurous leave.

Clark AFB, in the Philippines, was another one of my favorite bases to visit for a variety of reasons. It was a very active installation in the '68-'70 time period due to its position between Hawaii and Vietnam. I had been there many times, including the day and night in 1965 when we were on our way to Nha Trang with the 5th Air Commando Squadron, and again when I was required to attend the PACAF Jungle Survival Course (later in 1973). I had several occasions when I was glad to be there and one or two unpleasant ones.

One day, I was preparing for a test hop on one of our C-47s being completed by the 5200th Maintenance Wing for a such-and-such multi-hour inspection and maintenance. I checked the right wing aileron and as I was pushing it up, I heard a clunk, clunk, clunk, as something rolled from back to front. When I pulled the aileron down, I heard the same noise from front to back. As I looked closely at where the object had come to rest, I noticed a hole in the fabric that could only have been a bullet hole. This caused an obvious concern and delay while the maintenance troops made a further inspection but found no more bullet holes. This one had probably come down from Huk Mountain, just outside the downwind traffic pattern and which was supposedly controlled by Communist rebels. The offending 7.62mm round was extracted and the hole was patched in the canvas surface. As a Lt. Col. friend of mine, who was Base Ops Officer and was C-47 qualified remarked after we had been waiting under the wing of our Gooney Bird for two hours, "Lad, my Low-Liquor Level Light just came on, let's go to my house and have Martinis." Good idea, so we CNX-ed for MX and gave up our test hop for that day. The next day, after another test hop co-pilot joined me for the mission, we taxied out to the runway and started our take off roll. As we gained speed and just prior to lift off, I began to feel the rudder swinging back and forth. After gear up, the elevator started to pump the yoke up and down. The faster I went, the more pronounced the swings became. I turned to downwind leg, declared an emergency, and came in for a full-stop landing. Right after touchdown, No. 2 throttle lever came loose so I had to roll off the high-speed and shut down after calling for a tug—before anything else went wrong. When we jumped down and went around the tail, we found that most of the fasteners on the inspection plates on the rudder and elevator had popped and the plates had opened allowing the airstream to enter the control surfaces. Plus, a connecting bolt had dropped off the linkage thereby rendering it useless. We couldn't believe what we were looking at. The substitute co-pilot walked away and back to Base Ops muttering something about, "Boy, I don't know about you guys from Taiwan!" It wasn't our fault, though. The 5200th Maintenance Wing bit the bullet on that one. Evidently, the personnel felt bad about the incident because, before I headed back to Taipei, just days before my son was born, I received a really nice congratulation card signed by all the guys in the maintenance shop. It made me feel sorry that I had made such a stink about their shoddy maintenance.

The "Fillipinos" are very nice people until you are outside the Clark AFB gate, which I was on one occasion by myself. One of the really attractive waitresses at the O. Club had asked me to deliver a birthday present to her Father downtown, so, hoping that it would lead to more time spent with her afterwards, I agreed to follow her directions and deliver the present. When I boarded the colorful "Jeepney" outside the gate, there was already a local man aboard who greeted me cheerfully, saying, "Oh you know me, I'm Johnny from the BOQ Office." Well, I certainly didn't recognize him, and as I tried to exchange $5.00 US for Pesos, he tried to grab the money out of my hand. I held on to it with a tight grip, so tight that the Pesos tore in half as I bailed out of the "Jeepney" and ran into a bar on the sidewalk. The people inside were sympathetic, only because they had seen it many times before. When I was finally able to find the house to which she had sent me, I found her father rather amazed that I had made it there unharmed. He offered me a beer and then had his son accompany me all the way back to Clark AFB. He was grateful for the present I had found at the Base Exchange for his daughter to give him, although I can't remember just what it was, and I was grateful for the escort home. That was to the front gate where there are many local vendors under the watchful eyes of the Air Police gate guards. This is where I bought my blue velvet painting that I still have on display in my basement along with some other "treasures" from my Far East travels.

CHAPTER 12

AH SO-NUMBER ONE SON

It wasn't long after my return from the Philippines that Barbara and I were spending a Friday night at the O. Club, watching the Chinese guests gamble at one of the Las Vegas nights. I'm not sure how much the Chinese there knew about Las Vegas, but I am sure that the Chinese love to gamble. They would line up outside the Club waiting to gain entrance. As I was watching the frantic action at the tables and wheels, I had a friend come up to me and tell me that I needed to "report to the coat room!" When I arrived, I found my wife flat on her back on the counter with her pleated skirt above her knees, calling for me to take her to the hospital—STAT! Since she had only gained 15 or so pounds during her pregnancy, nobody knew she was that far along. We made it to the front lawn of the hospital where she exited our VW in a hurry, but only made it to the grassy area where her water broke. I ran in to grab someone to come outside and help her, thinking surely she was going to give birth right there. After everything, and I, calmed down, I was informed that I wasn't going to be a father for a few more hours. When the baby did finally come out, Barbara asked if it was a girl, and the doctor replied, "Not with that outdoor plumbing".

While in recuperation and recovery (R&R), the pediatric nurses brought the newborns to their mothers for the first time. As Barbara received a black-haired, almond-eyed bundle, she heard a scream from a Chinese mother who was yelling, "This no' my baby!" She was cuddling a blond-haired, blue-eyed cutie and obviously knew that it wasn't hers. The Chinese mother finally calmed down when my wife alerted the nurses for the obvious need for a switch of babies.

While I was assigned to MAAG Flight Operations, I was the most experienced C-47 operator. Therefore, I was on orders as PCP, FCF, IP, SEFE. My official title, according to my Joint Services Commendation Medal, was "Operations Staff Officer, Flight Operations Division, Air Force Section, Military Assistance Advisory Group, Republic of China. Not all the rated officers were C-47 qualified, so it fell to me as Passenger Carrying Pilot, Functional Check Flight, Instructor Pilot and Standardization Evaluation Flight Examiner to qualify non-Gooney Bird pilots in the "Douglas 'swept-wing' racer". Several of those qualification rides were memorable to say the least.

I had to give check rides and upgrades to pilots I didn't want to see in command, especially ones with limited reciprocating engine time and/or tail wheel experience.

About a month after one such upgrade, my current boss and I were doing some "Martini" scheduling at my house when I received a call on my notification number. When I answered it, the voice on the other end didn't say 'Boo, how are you, or where's the fire,' just uttered an "Ugh—followed by the question, "What's your definition of a ground loop?" All I could say was, "Oh, you didn't," as I snapped off the stem of my martini glass, --"was anybody hurt?" Well, it seems our inexperienced tail dragger novice had made it as far as Makung Island in the Formosa Strait and with a 30-40 knot tailwind had allowed the tail to rise to 20-30° degrees nose low and both props had contacted the concrete in the run-up area causing sudden engine stoppage and bending back all six blades. The inside propeller on No. 2 engine made close together nicks in the concrete and the blades on No. 1 engine on the outside of the turn made more widely spaced white grooves. Well, it took the Chinese Air Force with a C-119 or C-46 to bring the crew and passengers back home as well as ferry a maintenance crew with two new engines, two new props, engine stands out to Makung for the inevitable engine(s) change. But, guess who had to be flown out with copilot and Flight Mechanic to test hop our wounded bird? After 5 days out there on a Chinese Interceptor (F-104s) base, that was a sad –looking bunch of sunburned maintenance troops and they were itching to get home. But first, we had to test hop the two new engines, so they had to wait to see if their labors would be rewarded with a ride home. We did a very thorough pre-flight and engine run-up. When everything looked to be in the green, I ran the throttles up to 30", checked the gauges, and began take off roll. At about 50 knots, the Flight Mech. saw falling oil pressure on NO. 1 engine and called "ABORT!" With 10,000 feet of concrete or so, I had no trouble stopping and we taxied back for another try. The maintenance troops were crestfallen, but watched eagerly as we lined up for another try. The same thing happened again, and this time we shut down to see if we could diagnose the problem. That's when our Flight Mech. decided that if the oil quantity was even a quart low, it could cause the pressure indicator to fall during acceleration. We topped off the oil tank and the next take off was successful. I finished the FCF for both engines in less than an hour and returned to file while the "wrench-benders" loaded their gear. After a 7-Level Sergeant signed off the four or five red "X's" in the Maintenance form, we headed home. As we broke ground and leveled off to assure proper oil pressure, I heard cheering and clapping from the rear.

My immediate boss, Herb Dagg, was the primary pilot of the VC-54 that made good trips for the 2-star, to whom it belonged to Japan and Korea, like Cheju Do off South Korea and Baguio in the Philippines, both idyllic resorts that the lowly C-47 was never called upon to visit. Since he had flown both C-54s and C-47s during the Berlin Airlift, he was selected to re-qualify in the latter, which meant that I had to check him out. I didn't think it would take more than one training mission, so I filed local clearance and Herb and I proceeded to the airplane. Upon reaching our parking spot on the CAF ramp, he looked at our beautiful flying machine and remarked, "I can't fly this thing, it has two engines missing and the nose-wheel steering is on the wrong end!" But that was just the beginning. After he asked me to pull him up the 17 degree slope to the cockpit, he settled in the left seat and started on the checklist—SEAT AND RUDDER PEDALS, SEAT BELT AND SHOULDER HARNESS, FIRE EXTINGUISHER SWITCHES—standard BEFORE STARTING ENGINES stuff. He even recalled to which position the Hydraulic Pump selector went. Since Douglas Aircraft had produced both aircraft, there were some similarities between the C-54 and the C-47, despite the number of engines and the steering. Without going into detail about engine start, taxiing and run up, when we were cleared for take-off, I briefed on Emergency Procedures and we pushed the throttles forward and started down the runway. At about 60 knots, the Major folded his arms, took his feet off the rudder pedals and said, "I forgot!" Well, it didn't dawn on me at the time, but this wasn't as much as a checkout for him, but a kind of no-notice IP Proficiency Check for me. I was too busy lifting off, raising the landing gear, a two-step process on the floor and beside me, reducing power, turning out of traffic and going into a 500' overcast while continuing our right climbing turn to avoid the mountains only 10 miles away. When he finally decided to fly on his own, the rest of the mission was a piece of Egg Foo Yung. Of course we had to discuss engine limits, airspeeds and emergency procedures but he had accomplished his mission and I could sign him off as C-47 qualified. I don't think he ever flew a mission in his last three months before his rotation back to the States. Years later, I concluded that I wasn't giving him a check ride—he was testing me and my IP/FE capabilities.

Another pilot I was required to check out in the Gooney Bird had no multi-engine time. In fact, he was an ex-F-100 jockey who worked up in the Ops Shop with the Colonels and Generals. He had studied hard for his written exam and produced an almost perfect grade. Therefore, I thought he could handle just about anything I could present during his initial flight. He made good progress up to the take-off portion of the mission. With no one on final approach, we took the active and began take-off roll. Instead of saying "I forgot" at 60 knots, I pulled back No.2 throttle and hit the fire warning light. Without straying more than three feet off the center line, he pulled back the other throttle, unlocked the tail wheel and called for the ENGINE FIRE CHECKLIST while coasting smoothly off the high speed taxiway to our right. I called ABORT to the tower, gave him back No. 2 throttle and we taxied back for another normal, I promised him, take-off. I knew he was a natural-born pilot and even remarked as such on his evaluation form.

At the west end of Sung Shan CAFB, including Air Force Section MAAG Operations and the International civilian terminal, was the major maintenance facility for China Airlines. In addition to all the Boeing aircraft, 707, 727,747s that the airline owned and maintained, China Air had major maintenance contracts for all kinds of military aircraft, mostly those USAF types being flown in Vietnam. A USAF Lt. Col. Named Joe Sauressig was in charge of all these contracts, to see that the aircraft arrived on time, were given depot-level priority maintenance and repair, test flown and sent back to the theater in proper time and condition. Since he was somewhat understaffed pilot-wise, he called our Flight Ops looking for a loan of a test hop pilot. Since I was FCF qualified, it said so on my "Have Goon—Will Travel" calling card and was on official orders as such, I volunteered for the first requested test hop with Joe in a C-47. It turned out that this particular C-47 belonged to the VNAF (Vietnamese Air Force) and was "owned" by none other than "Big Minh", the large, cigar-smoking General who had regained power following the 1964 coup in Saigon. The distinguishing feature of this particular C-47, other than the yellow addition to the USAF star insignia, was the rocket canister nose cone that was screwed to the back of the copilot's seat, a big ash tray for "Big Minh's" cigar ashes.

Another test hop for which I was called was for a VNAF A-1E, a large, single-engine fighter/bomber adapted from the U S Navy. It had a four-man cockpit with room for two crewmembers under the rear, blue-tinted canopy. I had never flown anything like it since my T-28 days eight years earlier, but I was excited to go up with Joe to check out this single engine tail dragger with as much power in one engine as the Gooney Bird had in both. After all the power checks were made, we lined up for takeoff. Joe looked over at me in the right seat and asked if I was ready, then said, "Okay, you make the takeoff." The throttle was located between the seats, seemingly too small for such a big engine. As I eased the throttle forward, I was mindful of the great torque produced by the R-3350 engine and held in more rudder than even the T-28 required. As we approached 75 knots, I asked, "What is lift-off airspeed?" as we smoothly left the ground. My next question was, "What is climb airspeed?" We were doing were doing about 100 knots with gear and flaps up and Climb Power set, and Joe replied, "What you're doing is just fine." We spent about half an hour at 5500 feet checking out the engine, controls, avionics—all the things on the Functional Check Flight checklist, when Joe saw something below us and took control of the A-1E. He did a Split "S" and zoomed down to about 2000'. At about 220 knots, we pulled up alongside a Cathay Pacific Convair 880 and flew loose formation with him on final approach into Taipei International. We exchanged greetings with the surprised Cathay Pacific pilot and his left-side passengers. Then, Joe did a left wing-over and headed for the Tamsuei River below us, flew under the crossing power lines and called the tower for landing. Just like the T-34 in Alaska, we had to zoom up to traffic pattern altitude and downwind heading to fall in behind the Convair 880, only, this time, there was no "pants wetting". That was my last mission with Joe and China Air, but he wrote a very favorable endorsement for me that is still in my 201 File.

The third typhoon we experienced while living on Taiwan came up from the southeast and threatened all the military bases on the Island. Therefore, it was time to evacuate our USAF aircraft before the cyclone hit. I was assigned the delightful task of evacuating one of our C-47s to the Southwest to Clark AFB in the Philippines. It was, as one said in Chinese, "Mao Gwanchi", or "no sweat". Having flown near a typhoon, once going to Hong Kong, and once coming back, I was glad that I didn't have to experience another one. On the trip back to Taipei, John Jackson and I were returning to home port (the US Navy was the controlling agency on Taiwan) when we encountered rather severe turbulence approaching Sung Shan International. In order to keep on an even keel (Navy again), John, a football-player sized Captain, decided that he, in the Left seat, would control the rolling, pitching Gooney Bird down final approach by brute force on the controls, and that I, in the right seat would control the airspeed by manipulating the throttles so he could have both hands free to control the yoke in conjunction with the rudder pedals. It was all both of us could do to maintain a semblance of straight and level flight at 85-95 knots to touchdown, which John executed beautifully. Once under control on the runway, we heard applause and whistles from our passengers as we cleared the runway and taxied in, still gripping the yoke tightly to prevent tipping a la Makung. When we arrived at the Air Force Section Office, we heard the story about the evacuation of the VC-54 earlier to Kadena AFB Okinawa. It seems that Moe Harshbarger, (Major, 6' 4, 250 lbs, ex-football player and original member of the "Dirty Thirty" 1962 USAF/VNAF C-47 contingent at Tan Son Nhut), along with a rather diminutive, red-faced full Colonel, had departed Sung Shan in the '54 enroute to Kadena. While the Major was in command in the left seat, the 5'6" white-haired Colonel, who normally flew the assigned T-33 until John Jackson augmented an austere budget program that eliminated funding for the two-seat jet trainer, was trying to assist Moe with the controls in the on-coming turbulence of the approaching storm. While Moe was wrestling with the controls, the Colonel had a death grip on the yoke in the right seat, but all he could do was rise and fall, shoulder harness, seat belt and all, as the VC-54 rolled and pitched up and down, right and left. Finally, Major Moe called, "God Dammit, Col, get off the yoke, I've got it!" An hour later, they were safely on the ground at Kadena and glad to be behind the storm. During Post-Flight Inspection, maintenance found that 17 rivets had popped loose from the center wing section.

At this time, I had already reached my destination for the evacuation. The next day, I was able to call home (long before cell phones). When my wife asked how bad the weather was there, I said, "What weather? I've been at the O. Club pool for the last 2 hours. It's sunny and 85 here." Well, that didn't go over too well at home since the typhoon had taken out our yard fence and blown our banana trees all the way down the hill into the rice paddy below. There was some flooding locally for days afterwards. A couple of days later, I was on my way out to Sung Shan to greet the STAN/EVAL Contingent from 13th AF at Clark which had come for an inspection of the entire Air Force Section, including our Airlift Operations. They had arrived in a C-118, not as shiny as the "G-mo's", but certainly large enough to hold about 15-20 people plus all their baggage and equipment. Now, the only problem was how to move them all from the wet parking ramp to the Navy busses which had been requisitioned for their transport to the nearby hotel. In between was 6" to 18" of flood water. The flight crew solved the problem by breaking out the C-118's 20-man life raft and used it to ferry personnel and baggage to higher ground. From there, I led the busses through the flood zone in our green Volkswagen. When I came to the first turn, the VW didn't make the turn, it just floated straight ahead until it was about 20-30 feet out in a rice paddy. When it finally came to rest, I called for help from the guys on the buses. It only took four or five guys to push and pull the floating car back to dry ground and we proceeded on our way. I didn't know a Volkswagen would float until that day.

During their visit, I came due for an annual Proficiency Check. The only other C-47/C-54 Flight Examiner in the Pacific theater was Billy Chad. We had a proficiency flight scheduled during the week of their stay. Since this was also an R&R trip for some of the 13th AF personnel, Billy had brought his wife and they spent a night at Peitou, a resort spa just west of Taipei in the hills along the Tamsuei River. It was a delightful place to eat, drink get a "hotsie" bath and relax. Billy Chad was a very personable guy who got along wonderfully with everyone—especially the young girls and the Mama-san at the leading spa in Peitou. He was also a dead ringer for Brian Keith, the father on a popular stateside TV sitcom, *A Family Affair*. When he would visit the spa, all the girls would hover around "Uncle Bill". In black and white TV, the only style AFTN was in Taiwan, the blond hair was gray and he certainly acted fatherly toward the young girl attendants. So, when he arrived with his wife, he was greeted with a chorus of "Uncle Bill, Uncle Bill!" It took a lot of explaining to convince his wife about the resemblance, but she finally understood, since she was a *Family Affair* fan also. She had just never seen it in black and white.

If any of us had a drinking problem, the price of gin in Taiwan was of no help. I hadn't really liked Martinis until

I socialized with the folks stationed there on the Island.

Herb and Marie, our closest "socializers", introduced us to Herb's idea of a really dry Martini. He had cleaned out one of Marie's perfume atomizers and filled it with dry Vermouth. When he poured very cold gin into a Martini glass, he would merely "spritz" a spray of Vermouth over the top of the glass as he whispered, "Vermouth". Then he would add the best part, a small green "cocktail" tomato which was sold in the Navy Class Six store under the label: TOM OLIVES. If one were serving guests, the first Martini was with Beefeaters Gin and the rest were made with Millshire's. Millshire's was 50 cents a quart and Beefeaters was $4.00 a half-gallon. Herb always said that "Martinis were like a woman's breast—one's not enough and three's too many." After two of them, you couldn't tell if the gin was Beefeaters or Millshire's anyway. In order to serve the gin very cold, Herb had 6 or so frosted vials of about 3 or 4 ounces which he would fill with gin, Majors could afford the good stuff, put them in the freezer and by cocktail hour, they would be slushy and delicious. We also developed a taste for "Tanguaray 'Tinis" made with entirely different tasting gin. One had to acquire a taste for Tanguaray, but it was satisfying also.

When my Father and Mother-in-Law came to Taipei for our son's birth in late '68, we took them one Sunday afternoon to the O. Club and we all ordered Martinis. When 4 of them arrived, my Father-in-Law gave the "Shou-jeh" (waitress) $2.00 and received $1.20 in change. They were only 20 cents on Sundays. That $1.20 would almost have bought breakfast at the Club, where our dues were only $1.00 a month.

Now it was time for Barbara to take Burris and Sheesa to the US to her home in Wood River IL with her mother and father.

One night, I received a call at home asking me how long it would take to fly to Tainan and pick up a female dependent who had been bitten by a "Habu" (the Chinese equivalent of a Cobra.) I asked how long ago it had happened and if she was still alive. Two hours ago and it would take me an hour and a half more to fly down to Tainan, I said, "If she' still alive, you don't need me."

My Mother and Father also visited us in 1969 before taking Barbara, Burris and Sheesa to the States for a couple of weeks. While at our house to see his 9 month-old grandson, my Father sat with Burris while they listened to continuous quacking next door. Since Burris had been visiting next door for "Chinese Kindergarten" with Sheesa and some Chinese youngsters, they were using Mother Goose to teach the Chinese in English while Burris was learning a bit of Chinese. He therefore associated the wading birds next door with geese. When he heard them cackle, he told Grandpa that those were geese. After 3 or 4 attempts to correct him, my Dad finally said, "Burris, you have me firmly convinced that those are geese."

Barbara took Burris and Sheesa to her home in Illinois with her father and mother, leaving me with a 15 year old niece to keep me company for two weeks. Eng Oh didn't speak English and I didn't speak any Chinese or Taiwanese so we didn't communicate much, but her version of our living arrangement became clear the first night. When I was ready for bed, probably watching Lee Marvin in M Squad on black and white AFTN, in Chinese with English sub-titles, without a knock or voice prompt, here comes this cute little girl in a shorty nightie who jumped right in to bed with me and proceeded to snuggle her adorable body right up against me. It wasn't hard to get used to that kind of communication; however, there was a much-needed line not-to-be-crossed. It was hard not to, but we did it.

One of my flying buddies was the Base Operations Officer down-island at CCK (Chiang Chuan Kahn) AB. When he came to Taipei for a night, I invited him to the house for drinks and dinner. When he saw Eng Oh, he could tell about our arrangement. After I told him about the "limit", he understood and even confessed about his arrangement with his secretary Nancy at CCK.

Anyway, after a martini or two, it was time to eat Eng Oh's first dinner cooked at my house. She had fixed steak and potatoes with a vegetable and we thought it was going to be great. However, she had baked the steak to a well-doneness and it was terrible. Then and there, I told her from now on, I would cook my own food or eat out at the O. Club. At the end of two weeks, I was more than ready to have wife and child back, not to mention our most capable Amah, Sheesa.

I really relished my monthly trips to Hong Kong, not just to buy stereo equipment and clothing/jewelry, but to find the best places to eat and drink there. One such place was the Downstairs Bistro, an Australian eatery with charming waitresses and barmaids from "Down Under". The best meal and entertainment I had in Hong Kong was during an R&R with Barbara and my tailor, Mr. Vashi. He took us to the roof-top restaurant in the Hong Kong Hilton. He introduced us to Honey Dew Melon and Prosciutto as well as the legendary French entertainer Patichou. The view was over the Hong Kong harbor (harbour in Brit-spell), the food was fantastic and Patichou was entertaining. Despite my protests, Mr. Vashi paid for everything, explaining, "I have already made my first million, I don't care if I make a second million."

One day I was flying down-island with a Major from 13th Air force and we were sitting near the end of RWY 36 at CCK when "they launched the Ball Game" the full launch of the KC-135s for a few refueling missions of fighters and bombers into Vietnam. The weather was Delta Sierra, rain and low ceiling. Since the tankers were positioned on the north end of the field, and the wind was not a factor, yet, the tankers were roaring down Runway 18 right past us in position to take the other active 36. After one or two fully loaded 135's lifted off at the overrun, Jerry said to me, "Jackes, I want to see the look on your face the first time you're 10,000 feet down a runway and still on it." I replied, "Never gonna happin." Two months later, I received my orders to SAC in KC-135s.

CHAPTER 13

WHERE DO THEY PUT ALL THAT FUEL?

After two blissful years without a Chinese-Communist take-over from the Mainland, a serious traffic accident or a violent earthquake, it was time for our next PCS (Permanent Change of Station). During my whole career to this point I had deliberately annotated my "Dream Sheet", or Assignment Preference Statement, with the statement: "Definitely do not desire assignment to SAC." It was now time to find out where and to what we were going. Congratulations, Jackes, you're going to SAC—to KC-135s. The only good news was that the assignment base was Ramey AFB in Puerto Rico. When I came home with the news, Barbara asked me, "What language do they speak there?" I assured her that English was spoken there along with Spanish, which was a lot easier to learn than Chinese.

So, we prepared for a new life in a new place, flying a new airplane. Since I had never seen the inside of a KC-

135, I was scheduled for upgrade at March AFB in Merced California for three months. But first we had to unload some of the items that either the Air Force wouldn't ship or that we couldn't get the "Buy-Sell" man to take off our hands. He was a bit of local color who would come up our hill periodically with his motorcycle cart and ring his bell. When someone would come to the door, he would grin, showing his big gold front tooth and ask, "You have anything to sell?" Usually, Sheesa would chase him away, but one time we were able to palm off a broken television console that didn't have any picture, but we plugged it in and showed that it lit up at least. Since there wasn't any picture, we told him that there wasn't any program on that early in the day. He bought that, but didn't give us much for the set. I'm sure he had it fixed, since it was probably "made in Taiwan" anyway, and sold it for an exorbitant price, but we just wanted to get rid of it. We had also acquired a lot of booze and exotic mixes, so we had a "clean out the bar" party so we would not have to pour it out. It was illegal to give it away to the Chinese, and the Government wouldn't ship it for us. We had our beautiful teakwood bar all set up, hired an enlisted man to tend bar and Sheesa made her "famous" Cheese Surprises—deep fried wontons around an ingot of sharp cheese with a hot green pepper on top inside. It was very tasty with the melted cheese and "Surprise!" The pepper comes through. We invited everybody we knew in the US Military community. The house was crowded and there was no more parking to be had. Everyone had a good time but only drank Gin, Bourbon and Scotch—no Mai-Tis, Tequila Sunrises, Pina Colladas, all the things we wanted to get rid of.

Right after we arrived, at least within the first year, we had our car "chopped" for some outlandish fee by a Taiwanese who was in the newspaper business and was willing to wait over a year to buy our little green Volkswagen. Therefore, he put his "chop" on a bill of sale until it was time for us to leave Taiwan. Then he would honor his "chop", pay the agreed sum and he would own the car. We also had no trouble finding a buyer for our refrigerator/freezer, a highly valued stateside appliance. Sheesa and her husband came up with enough money to pay almost as much as a new one would have cost through the Navy Exchange. So, now, during our relocation from Taiwan to Puerto Rico, we would need a new car and a refrigerator/freezer.

Our trip home was somewhat more eventful than the one over to Taiwan in 1968 since this time we had an under two year old to keep track of on the 747. In addition to all our carry-ons, we had a bag full of toys plus a few snacks and juices for Burris. Fortunately, the airline gave us front row coach seats with added leg room so we could have more room for all our "stuff". Well, Burris decided that that was <u>his</u> space and was using it all for 5 ½ hours during which he ran up and down the aisle, generally making a nuisance of himself, but since most of the fellow passengers were military and families of their own, they didn't object too much to his behavior, but it wore us out trying to calm him down. No matter what we did, nothing worked. Finally, about 45 minutes before landing, he finally conked out. Now, we had to carry a sleeping 20 month old off the airplane and hope he stayed that way until we could get some rest.

Before moving to our new island paradise, we were able to return to our "roots", St. Louis and Wood River. We had no trouble finding baby sitters for Burris with both sets of grandparents wanting equal time with their grandson. Our first concern was buying a new car. My dad had already bought my first two cars, my '53 Merc and my '55 Studebaker. The first, a cute little 2-door sedan, dark green metallic with a stick shift, I nearly totaled by my foolish notion that the big mail truck coming from my left with his right turn blinker on was actually going to turn right. Instead, he plowed right into me just aft of the driver side door, bending the frame. That was a really sweet car which I drove for a while after it was realigned in a truck frame straightening rig. When it was time to graduate from St. Louis Country Day, and move to college at Washington University, a lot closer to home than I wanted, it was time to upgrade to a Studebaker Commander. Loved that car and wish I still had it—black with wire wheels, a spot light, leopard skin floor mats and the "V" bar out of the nose so it looked like an F-100.

This time, my Dad suggested a new car from a dealer friend of his. Since we had already had an American Motors car, the Rambler convertible in Oklahoma and California, which Sue won in the 1962 divorce, the new inspiration from American Motors was a 70 ½ Gremlin, a compact, sawed-off 6 cylinder coupe with a stick shift, bench seats, white with a red interior and a red stripe along the side. It was very practical and would certainly get me from St. Louis to California and back plus be economical in Puerto Rico. I didn't know how much we'd be driving there but I was warned that the car would probably rust after two years that close to the ocean, so I had it double undercoated before we shipped it to Puerto Rico.

During my long drive from Illinois to California in my brand new *Gremlin,* everywhere I stopped for gas I would be asked, "What kind of a car is <u>that</u>?" I would say, "That is a 70 ½ *Gremlin.*" Since nobody west of St. Louis had ever seen one before, they'd be looking at the odd shape and ask, "What happened to the back end?" Anyway, it made it to Merced in good time with plenty of good gas mileage.

CHAPTER 14

WELCOME TO SAC

I had to report in to the 93rd Air Refueling Squadron, process in and find a place to live during upgrade training in the KC-135. I found a small apartment in a motel just outside the main gate that catered to just such students as I. It was adequate for me as I'm sure it had been for hundreds of previous occupants. I had a bed, shower and kitchen with a hot plate, stove and refrigerator—everything I needed for bachelor living.

Now it was time to become acquainted with my new aircraft. Since I had only viewed a KC-135 from a distance, I had no idea what to expect. During our introductory walk-around at the beginning of ground school, I was certainly impressed by the size of the sleek 4-engine aircraft. As we climbed up the crew ladder to the cockpit, I was equally impressed not only by the complexity of the instrument panel and overhead radio/electrical panel, but by the comparative roominess of the forward station where the four crewmembers had seats. When we went through the Nav. Compartment bulkhead aft, I was completely amazed by the cavernous cargo compartment. Where the 707 had had 120 or so seats, there was nothing but empty space all the way back to the tail. With the cargo door open, it looked like a C141 cargo plane. My immediate question was, "Where does all the fuel go?" The answer was, "Under the floor, Forward Body, Center Wing and Aft Body tanks, plus a reserve in the Upper Deck Tank." I would soon become very familiar with all these as the Co-Pilot's main responsibility during refueling was maintaining the balance of all those tanks to keep the center of gravity within limits. I also had to learn the other intricacies of the complicated Boeing *StratoTanker,* which I never really did in the two years I flew it.

Boy, the first time we climbed aboard for our first training mission! I'll never forget the feeling of power and speed as I completed the Before Takeoff Checklist. With four J-57 jet engines and water injection, we went from 0 to rotation to lift off before I could catch my breath from the sudden acceleration after I actuated the water injection switches on the Co-Pilot's panel. At the required airspeed, the IP rotated the nose wheel off the runway and seconds later we were airborne and climbing out. It was not quite as thrilling as the F-100 ride at Homestead and a lot noisier than the WB-50, but really impressive for an aircraft that heavy and much more exciting than most of my previous C-47 runway departures. Gear Up, accelerate to Climb Speed, Water Shut Off, Flaps Up and we were off and running. I thought anything over 500 feet per minute and 10,000 feet at 240 knots would give me a nose bleed, but I managed to follow through on the After Take Off and Climb Checklist and actually have time to see the California countryside including Yosemite Park passing under our right wing tip and the Imperial Valley; a regular sight-seeing tour. But I was snapped back to reality when asked if I was following the **FRIANT TRANSITION** on this Standard Instrument Departure (SID). I had to admit I was a little bit behind, understandably, but I managed to find the next NAVAID frequency and enter it in the overhead panel VOR-DME radio. Now it was my turn to fly. Just follow the Departure, with a little help, level off at FL230 (23,000'), after putting on my helmet and oxygen mask as we passed 18,000'. We had all been briefed on the procedure, but it still seemed foreign to me, having never been in a 4-engine jet tanker before where things moved a lot faster than they had in the WB-50 where, if we had to go to 18,000' (500 milibars) or even 30,000' (300 mb), we had plenty of time to prepare. After our initial check out, oxygen masks were only required before refueling. (But that's a later story.)

Enter, the "Simulator"—an airplane-like reproduction of a real KC-135. It was a far cry from the LINK boxes that attempted to simulate the B-25 and B-50 at

McClellan, certainly not the real life feel of a real airplane, but good for instrument approaches and emergency procedures. The NCO outside the contraption could put a student pilot in all kinds of dangerous conditions like engine failure on takeoff, fire, fuel leak, control failure—all things hard to make happen during real flight without endangering the crew or the aircraft. Fortunately, I had learned the FRIANT TRANSITION from Castle AFB to the Military Operation Area (MOA) of the day's mission before I actually had to do it for real in the KC-135. In ground school I tried to master the many complexities of a very complicated airplane deigned to refuel all other types of aircraft from F-104s to B-52s. Also taught in ground school was the process of air refueling, but the only way to really learn it was to actually do it. It's a precise, demanding procedure, but really fun to do and satisfying to accomplish when everything goes by the book. The school also teaches "Autopilot-Off" refueling which really tests your handling skills.

One item that was taught in Tanker Ground School was Flash-blindness Protection. In the eventuality of a nuclear detonation visible from a tanker, we were taught about aluminum foil curtains to cover the windows and an eye patch which could cause a crew member to lose sight only in one eye allowing the pilot or co-pilot to see with the covered eye during refueling following a nuclear detonation. About the second time I heard this lecture and practice, I asked, "Has any of you ever <u>seen</u> a nuclear detonation?" "Of course not—have you? I told them about the 2 or 3 I had witnessed on Christmas Island. They may have thought I was a "smart-ass" but had to admit that I knew a lot more about flash blindness than they did. When it came to how the shock waves would affect the autopilot, everyone took notice. That fact had been left out of the lesson plan.

After completing the required familiarization training in the KC-135, it was time to officially join the Command that I had so specifically requested not to join. As soon as I arrived at the 91st Air Refueling Squadron at Ramey AFB Puerto Rico, I was assigned an aircrew and became an Aircraft Commander, since I had over 5000 hours flying time. Of course, since SAC had made me one, they expected me to act like one, which wasn't going to be easy. I only had 25 or 30 hours in the unfamiliar "beast" and now I was the Commander of a 4-man crew and all the responsibility that went with it. Since this was SAC and during the Cold War, I was expected to know and be able to brief on any mission that could be called for under wartime conditions. Everything was classified and we all had to be able to recite all the steps and procedures to take if the "balloon went up". I soon found out that I had better read and heed all the pertinent rules and regulations as well as SAC Supplements thereto that governed SAC aircrews and their mission. I also developed a yen to repaint the big sign just inside the main gate near the runway end that said: "Peace Is Our Profession." I really thought it should read: "Peace Is a Sour Profession."

First was the charming little chore of spending an entire week cooped up in a windowless facility during "Alert". There, with 3 other crews, 1 KC-135 and 2 B-52, we lived in isolation studying, briefing, eating, sleeping and occasionally, hearing that obnoxious Klaxon going off so we could run out to our aircraft and exercise our quick-start capability either up to engine start, to pre-taxi, to taxi to takeoff, to Abort and return to our parking spot depending on what the Command Post ordered. One scenario included max power up to refusal speed, throttles to idle and taxi back so we could then re-cock our tanker and get ready to do it another time. This was as close to the real thing as it could be without actually taking off and proceeding on your mission. You never knew what level the alert scramble would attain, but take off roll was really exciting and you had better do it by the numbers or there was Hell to pay with a formal de-briefing in front of the Director of Operations (DO)—an unforgiving full Colonel second in command only to the Wing Commander.

My flying career in SAC was certainly less than outstanding. I never had the same Co-pilot, Navigator or Boom Operator twice in a row. I'd have one crew for alert, but a different one for the next mission. I finally painted a hole on the back of my helmet with a tapered piece of wood sticking out of it and the title: "Square Peg". One reason for the low placement on the mission crew board was that every other check-ride was a re-qual.

During my first mission with a Stan/Eval pilot in the right seat, everything went by the book for a heavyweight takeoff and climb to 28,000'. Then I noticed during our NW route to the Refueling Area that No. 3 engine oil pressure kept going below the green area. As I reduced power on it, the pressure returned but then dropped off again. The check pilot asked me what I was going to do, so I pulled the throttle to idle cut-off and called for Engine Failure Checklist. Now I had to decide what to do next so I started a turn back to Ramey and notified Miami Center that I was going to return to base. Now, the Major on my right notified me that I had better do one of two things—either lighten the load or go down, since our airspeed was 3 knots above the stall and we were still at FL280. I had him notify Center that we were descending and declaring an emergency. I also began dumping fuel so we wouldn't have a lot on landing. The Flight Examiner also informed me that I needed permission from SAC HQ at Offitt to dump all that fuel, so I asked him if he could do that so I could concentrate on having the Navigator give me a new heading to Ramey, tuning in the VOR and ILS for approach and have the Boom Operator figure how much fuel to dump for proper landing weight and to figure out approach speeds for 3-engines. While I also monitored the fuel panel to make sure our CG stayed in balance, I changed the radio channel to Ramey Approach Control and requested a straight-in ILS approach. By now, we had permission to dump fuel, had our landing weight, approach speeds figured, gear down, flaps set,— now all I had to do was get us on the runway. I had never actually landed with an engine inoperative. In training, SAC procedure called for the simulated failed engine to be returned to power at 300 feet for a go-around, but this was real. Besides that, the wind was no longer down the runway, but had become a slight tailwind. I was trying, as usual, to make a smooth landing, but as I felt for the ground, the aircraft kept drifting to the left and was floating in ground effect due to the light weight, about 70,000 lbs. lighter than at take- off. By the time I finally touched down, softly, the left edge of the runway was no longer visible out my window and only half of the runway remained. I flunked the ride as the Examiner wrote: "Landing was unsafe." After that, I had to have a remedial training mission. In fact, every other mission was a "Re-qual".

Alert was not only a pain because you were not at home for seven days without going anywhere, but because you had to live with B-52 "Pukes"—a fighter pilot term. They were a different breed altogether, especially the Gunners. Fortunately, we didn't have to associate much with them since there was great rivalry between tanker and bomber folks. During one ORI (Operational Readiness Inspection), my crew wasn't on alert, but it became our job to guard the booze and food for the bomber crews because after alert launch of most of the tankers and "BUFFS" (Google that), the tankers would return after 4 or 5 hours from their refueling tracks and the bombers wouldn't return until they had flown for 8 or so hours following their simulated bomb run and low-level route. Therefore, it was up to us to assure that there was rum and roast beef still available for them.

From alert at Ramey, we were dispatched up to Goose Bay Labrador for a cold, snowy week on "Reflex Alert". First, we had to fight our way up there. The weather forecast was for 15-20° degrees below zero with winds of 20+ knots. About half way to our frigid alert location, the Navigator realized that the local winds were in True heading and since Goose Bay was so close to the Magnetic North Pole, not where Santa and the elves live and work, the variation from True North to Magnetic North would put the crosswind component way past our landing threshold. Therefore, we had to land at Pease AFB in Massachusetts and await a shift in the wind direction at Goose Bay. We checked into the BOQ and tried to get some sleep before starting our crew day all over. Just about the time we dozed off, the call came to saddle up and head on to Goose Bay. Somehow, the aircrew managed to land safely in the dark and snowy gloom. When we de-planed and started to unload our baggage, the icy wind actually took your breath away. The temperature was -20 and the wind was 30 knots, giving a wind chill of around -50° degrees. What a place to spend a week! The alert facility was half-buried in the snow and the entrance was actually underground.

About the third day on alert, we had accomplished our daily chore of going out to our designated A/C that had all our cold weather gear at the ready when we received the alert call and rushed out to our bird. The alert message called for immediate engine start, which meant firing off the black powder charge on No. 4 engine to get it up and running on its own ASAP, then pushing up the throttle to 90% and "gang-load" the other 3 starter switches. I thought the No. 4 cartridge had fired, but I only saw 9 or 10% RPM on the gauge, so I called for air so I could start normally. As soon as I heard, "You got air!" I squeezed together the toggle switches and Surprise! That was for cartridge start, not normal start. As soon as that hot air from the ground starter unit hit the unburned starting cartridge, the RPM shot to 80-90% and I was able to start the other three engines. After the exercise was over, Maintenance had to check the engine that I had started so abnormally. They found that the starter had been shredded and when the cowling was removed, pieces of the starter fell down on the icy ramp below. That didn't exactly endear me to the powers that be. It meant that we were "Non-effective" as an alert crew until the aircraft was back on "Alert Ready" status—about half a day after a new starter was installed, tested and declared O/R (Operational Ready). It also meant we could leave the alert facility for a little R&R at the O. Club and chat up some of the school teachers, without any alcohol of course.

The next big event during our week's stay at beautiful Goose Bay was another engine start exercise— this time for snow clearing of the ramp area behind all the alert birds. The plows had pretty well kept up with the runway and taxiway clearing, but now it was time to clear out all the walls of snow that had piled up behind the Alert Ramp. We had normal starting sequence, not an alert start, but even though I had all 4 engines running, about half of the alert fleet could only start 2 or 3 engines. We all were able to taxi forward so the plows could begin. After the plows were finished, some of us were able to taxi back, but one or two decided to be towed back to the alert parking ramp. My thoughts were, "Boy, I'll bet the Russians are really scared of this bunch!"

While I was at Ramey AFB in the tropical Caribbean, the weather was warm and wonderful. There were many opportunities to enjoy such. One such day, I was on the golf course in my multi-colored slacks about as far as one can be from the Clubhouse, when one of the almost daily afternoon thunderstorms cropped up and put an end to golf for a while. I jumped into my golf cart and headed for the cover of the Pro Shop. When I arrived, soaking wet and dripping, the DO, Col. John Mash, had already sought refuge and took one look at my soggy red, blue, yellow and green pants and said, "God, I hope those don't fade."

Right after we arrived at Ramey, the former occupant of our quarters at 601 B 6th Street, named Leon Tucci, sold me his 150cc *Lambretta* motor scooter for about a Dollar per cc. It was great for getting around the base. I painted it Air Force blue and silver, bought a helmet for Burris who was only 2 ½ but could stand in front of me and tool around the base with me. My favorite place was the O. Club with the beautiful view of the ocean and its *Cuba Libres*. Burris put up with my forays because the bartender would supply him with maraschino cherries. His favorite place was the swimming pool. He had no fear of water—the Lifeguard used to call him "Tadpole". If I ever went to the pool by myself, which wasn't very often, he would always ask, "Where's Tadpole today?" One day, Barbara and I took our eyes off him for about 10 seconds and when we heard a yell, I saw Burris jumping off the diving board. When I saw him sinking in the deep end I jumped in too. There he was in 9 feet of water, eyes wide open, blond hair streaming upward and a smile on his face. I pushed him up to the surface where the Lifeguard grabbed him and pulled him out. When I surfaced, Burris saw me and jumped right back into my arms like he always did when he was learning to swim.

We took him to see "Tora, Tora, Tora" at the Base Theater one evening. After about 30 minutes, when the Japanese airplanes were taking off to bomb Pearl Harbor,

Burris stood up and exclaimed, "My daddy flies airplanes!" We had to take him out of there—it was time for his nap.

On Friday nights, I used to like to watch Friday Night Fights, boxing matches, on AFTN. I would usually have a couple of Screwdrivers with some Fresca, while Barbara tried to put Burris in his crib and get him to go to sleep. It became a ritual of trying to get him to calm down so we could have a peaceful night, but it never happened. He would climb out of his crib and go to the door, start crying and jerk on the door handle until either we went to bed ourselves, ignoring his protests, or let him out of his bedroom and entertain him until he finally went to sleep, usually well past our bedtime.

The living quarters at Ramey were not only mandatory—there was no off-base housing—but also utilitarian. All the Company Grade and below was concrete block with a flat roof with a decent lawn and jalousie windows. Security was not a problem since only base personnel had access to the neighborhoods, so nobody had to lock the doors. One unbreakable regulation was that the house into which you were moving had to be as clean and neat as it was before you moved in. When we had to replace a broken refrigerator, about two months after we arrived, we pulled out the old one that had gone "toes up" and found quite a mess behind it—kids toys, pieces of broken dishes and dirt in the form of dust balls and sand behind the old unit; so much for the formal inspection of the previous tenants. When we (I) left, the standard method of cleaning was conducted—move all the Government furniture out on the lawn, close all the jalousies and bring in a fire hose to blast all the surfaces clean. Of course, mildew was a problem, so heater/driers had to be used to dry out the house. Fortunately, we were gone before the cleaning process began at 601B 6th Street.

When we arrived at Ramey, there were rumors that the base would be closing soon as part of the BRAC, Base Realignment And Closure, program. At a base wide orientation program, the Base Commander assured all of us that as soon as he knew anything, he would make it known to us. Six months later, he read "RAMEY CLOSING" in his San Juan *Star* one Sunday morning at his breakfast table. We received the news shortly after he did and two months later, our tour at Ramey was over.

Fortunately, I had decided to celebrate our 5th wedding anniversary with a cruise around the Caribbean. I had made all the arrangements with the on-base travel office and we were able to stash Burris with the Family Center with a great deal of acrimony on both Barbara and Burris's part, but our neighbors offered to help check up on him and off we went. The ship was the *Carla C,* of the Costa Line. It was a single stacker with only about 300 passengers—not like the *Costa Concordia* of Italian disaster fame. We both had a marvelous time, away from SAC, Burris and Alert.

The first night, right after we boarded and found our stateroom, I headed up to the bow and let the cool ocean breeze dry my sweat as we cleared the San Juan harbor and headed out to sea. Then I joined Barbara at the bar—I knew where to find her—that was kept open until we were well out to sea. We had a nightcap or two before dropping off to sleep in our gently rolling bunk. We only had one whole day of cruising at sea enroute to Caracas Venezuela and I took to the pool for fun and games (and a very lovely lady from Cleveland). We were playing games in the pool like who can dive down to the bottom and come to the surface with the most silverware that had been dumped into the deep end. There must have been another game or two because I still have two chintzy little trophy cups from the <u>Carla C</u>.

We had five different stops in each port-of-call after Caracas and everywhere we went we heard the ubiquitous steel drums, which are novel and melodious, but which begin to get really old after 5 or 6 times hearing them. They were everywhere. I even bought a small one to take home for a toy for Burris. At the stop on Martinique, or somewhere, I was wearing my loud golf slacks and the musicians were "rapping" about "De mon in de fancy pants, must want to find romance". While we were ashore, we did some shopping and returned to the ship with two sporty and really expensive-looking watches. They seemed to be real bargains. So, back on board, we wore our new prizes to the bar and asked the bartender, "Would you believe we bought these for only $75 each?" When he looked somewhat amused and shook his head, we said "$50?" Again, the head shake. When we said, "$45 for both?" He looked smug and said, "That's more like it," and walked away. They sure looked expensive, but by the time we returned to Ramey, they had already started turning green and had stopped working altogether.

We had some visitors during our brief stay in Puerto Rico. My sister and brother-in-law decided to fly down from Missouri and have a little vacation with us. They called us to find out how far it was from San Juan to Ramey and I told them it was 3 hours. She said, "No, how _far_ is it?" I said again, "Three hours," thinking they would rent a car and drive the north coast road through Aguadilla to the Base. When they thought about the three hour drive, they decided it would be faster and easier to fly PRINAIR to Mayaguez instead. PRINAIR flew multi-colored De Havilland Doves to all the smaller airports around Puerto Rico. Each one had its own solid color—sky blue, mauve, peach or mint green, etc. As Barbara and I waited at the airport at Mayaguez, we drank Pina Coladas and took bets on what color the next Dove would be. After about 4 arrivals and Pina Coladas, my sister and brother-in-law finally arrived. I don't remember the color, but my Sister wasn't very impressed with the airplane. "If I had known it was bolted together in the middle and the Steward was also the Co-Pilot, we'd have driven." By the time we arrived at Ramey, she was glad they hadn't challenged the roads after all.

The next day, Al and I took to the golf course for a round while the girls did whatever girls do—go to the pool with Burris. Al was a pretty good golfer, but he'd always played in the Midwest where the closest water was a small lake or pond. When he started to line up his putt on #2 green, I reminded him that the ball would be breaking toward the Ocean. He didn't believe me and his putt missed the cup by 3', toward the Ocean. He believed me on #3 and curled it right in.

I had some interesting missions during my two years as an Aircraft Commander, even if I wasn't a very good one.

During one of my first air-refueling missions out of Ramey AFB, I had the privilege of refueling four F-104's with the Puerto Rican Air National Guard. They were flown by US pilots and required a drogue on the KC-135 boom for connection with the probe on the F-104.

As we entered the refueling area, the "hot shot" pilots in their sleek supersonic fighter-interceptors were having a little trouble finding the drogue, so by the time we were at the end of the area, I called lead, in contact position, but not yet in contact, and told him that I was going to make a 180° left turn and he should "hang on".

He lit his afterburner, rolled down and right, and executed a nifty barrel roll over the top of us, settling right back into contact position. "Now, go ahead and make your God Damn 180° turn." Cool!!!

B-52 - I took this picture over the Gulf of Mexico from the window of the boom pod with a polarizing filter. The B-52 was enroute to the SAC Bomb Completion with a new paint job (note the white tape around the windows) and a big 2 on the tail with a gold wing and the motto: Second to None. Number 5 engine is seen in the upper left.

We were sent up to a refueling area in Montana where the prevailing winds were westerly and strong just south of the Canadian Border. As we established contact with the B-52 receiver, his Navigator warned us about the Jet Stream winds at our refueling altitude. He was going to be early and we may be late for the rendezvous. The refueling maneuver had us at FL280 westbound about 5 miles north of the racetrack pattern IP (Initial Point). The B-52 was inbound to the CP (Contact Point) heading East. With the Air-to-Air TACAN counting down the miles between us at a slant range and bearing, my Navigator shouted, "Push 'em up and turn left NOW!" I banked through the 180° degree turn at 28,000' and rolled out over the IP heading East with the receiver right behind us at 27,000', almost in Pre-Contact position. With a 100 knot wind at refueling altitude, the B-52 was almost 200 knots faster than we were. He saw us through the turn and couldn't believe we rolled out 1000' above him, on refueling heading and ready for off-load. He came up 1000', requested clearance to Contact Position and in 2 to 3 minutes, we were "passing gas". Now we had to turn left in the pattern before we exceeded our boundary. We had a lot more time on the upwind leg so things calmed down a lot. The Bomb Wing Commander was on board the BUFF and radioed, "I don't' know how we did this, but we're not going to do it the same way tomorrow!"

The KC-135 had a water injection system that was able to pump 5583 gallons of water through the four J-57 engines to increase power on takeoff by 15 to 20 %. When the fuel is well below wartime max, the temperature and Pressure Altitude is low enough, the aircrew has the prerogative to take off without the water. It saves about 30,000 lbs of take-off weight—at least for the 120 seconds it takes to run through the engines.

At Davis-Montham AFB, in Arizona, we were waiting for our A-10 receivers to depart their home base and head for the refueling area. I had elected not to fill the water tanks, thanks to the mission planners, because we weren't that heavy and the weather was nice and cool. As we waited and waited, with engines running, for word from the Command Post that our A-10 were airborne, the temperature was going up as was the Pressure Altitude. Since we were already at 5300' elevation, we only had about 5 or 6 degrees to go before the temperature, Pressure Altitude and fuel weight would require us to shut down and fill the water tanks. Just about the time the tower gave us our latest temperature, the Command Post called to launch—receivers up and running. We were within 2 degrees of our max temperature. We used almost all the runway before lifting off, but the charts were correct and the "Pucker Pressure" subsided as soon as we had Gear Up.

The most interesting mission stateside was one to refuel the 33rd TAC Fighter Wing F-4s that had been on a cold weather exercise in Alaska and were ready to return to Homestead AFB in Florida. We had to orbit south of Anchorage for almost an hour before the F-4s departed Elmendorf AFB for their homeward bound long flight with one refueling down the road in Washington State. The F-4s are very agile and easy to refuel, so no problem was anticipated. The third bird kept disconnecting and couldn't receive fuel. After 4 or 5 attempts, my Boom Operator, my favorite "Square Peg" crewmember, came up on interphone and asked if I wanted to lock the boom into the F-4's receptacle. That way, contact could be maintained throughout the whole off-load. He also informed me that it was strictly against regulations because, if a breakaway was necessary, the nozzle would break off and stay in the F-4's receptacle. Everyone decided it was worth the risk, so the Boom Operator pulled the circuit breaker on his panel that would allow the boom to lock in the slot and hold until the receiver was full. It worked like a charm. We had advised #3 what we were doing and that there would be no breakaway, but he and the other three F-4s agreed that it would work and allow them to fly on home rather than abort to another base to fix the problem. They all thanked us for our "can-do" attitude and I even received a (non-specific) thank you from the 33rd TAC FTR Wing Commander.

One particular incident had endeared that particular Boom Operator to me. Ray was walking on base in his flight suit. He had just exited the chow hall, talking to a friend, and had not yet donned his flight cap. When an officer passed, both saluted, but the officer stopped Ray and asked where his hat was. "It's in my pocket, Sir." "Why isn't it on your head, Sergeant?" "Because I can't get my head in my pocket, Sir." Then he reached down, pulled out his hat, put it on, saluted and kept on walking.

As I mentioned before, in the Davis-Montham mission, the KC-135 had 5583 gallons of water available for take-off to boost the power of the 4 J-57 engines for 120 seconds.

Well, for an air show demonstration for some unknown dignitaries—probably the ones who decided to close Ramey AFB, I was co-piloting for the big Captain who wore the "SAC SUX" patch on his sleeve and whom shall remain nameless unless I have already divulged his name, size and attitude. He was an Instructor Pilot for the 91st Air Refueling Squadron, and a real "fun guy".

We were only scheduled to make a low pass over the Base at 1500 feet so the DVs could have a good view of our typical tanker aircraft. Having decided to make a dry take-off, we still had water on board. As we headed down the runway for our nice little 1500 foot pass, Warren started the throttles forward while requesting that I "Hit the water, Jackes!" Boy, what a kick, as we climbed almost straight up for 6000 feet! I think everybody except the DO and Commander had a thrill.

CHAPTER 15

BACK STATESIDE AGAIN

When it came to moving from Puerto Rico to Wichita Kansas, Barbara and her father decided that a trip to Russia was much more fun and educational than moving. I managed to keep everything on schedule for the movers, house cleaners, squadron duty, and even had time for a visit from the Castle AFB Base Commander's secretary for a day or two in San Juan. That was the only pleasant part of the week or so it took to accomplish a PCS move. I hadn't found out just what to do with my old *Lambretta* motor scooter, but one of my Boom Operators took care of that for me. I told him he didn't have to load it on a KC-135, strapped to a bulkhead, but right after I said that, I saw it going up the ramp through the cargo door and I was assured that I would find it among the various equipment items being transferred to McConnell. So, when I arrived a week later, there it was, way over on the side of the Maintenance

Hangar. I think I bought him a bottle of cognac for that kind deed. I was even able to have it shipped to Wood River IL in 1974 where I rode it a few times, but it required too much maintenance and I sold it at a garage sale.

Now it was time to put all this training into practical use. Here comes "Young Tiger"—the deployment of KC-135s and B-52s to augment the air armada deployed against North Vietnam. Our Tanker Task Force was stationed at U-Tapao RTAFB in Thailand along with a squadron of B-52s. They didn't need our refueling, their fuel load allowed them to fly from southern Thailand to North Vietnam and back without refueling, but there were many fighters and other assorted USAF aircraft that did need our refueling. Rather than flying all B-52 missions out of Guam, there were a dozen or so bombers on alert at U-Tapao which could reach a target in two hours or less, rather than the 5 or 6 from the island base. We, on the other hand, were up in northern Thailand and the Gulf of Tonkin to provide refueling for fighter/bomber strikes almost within sight of the targets. A typical mission was to set up an orbit in a Refueling Anchor—Red, Yellow, Silver, Purple etc., and wait for a flight of F-4s—Ford Flight, Chevy Flight, Olds Flight—top them off before they headed to target, then wait for them to return for post-strike refueling and hope we counted the same number going home as we did coming in. The post-strike refueling was always quicker and quieter, only 5 or 6000 lbs of go-home fuel and debrief about the strike and what happened to anyone who didn't come out. When we hear, "One, Two, (silence), then Four" we knew it would be a somber rejoin. I only lost one in the 60 days of my tour. That was the only part of refueling that wasn't enjoyable and fulfilling. During one of our 0-dark thirty morning briefings, the Chaplain remarked: "Of course, if Charlie really wanted to stop the bombing, all they'd have to do is knock down the tankers." That thought stayed with us for a long time, especially up in the Gulf of Tonkin where we could almost see where the missiles would be coming from.

One day we were up in Yellow, or some color anchor, waiting and waiting for anything that needed fuel, when my Boom Operator called and said, "We've got one behind us and I think he needs fuel." I asked, "One of ours or one of theirs?" He told me it was an F-105 with a hole big enough for a man to stand up in in the left wing root. Obviously, he was desperate for fuel, but was NODO, No Radio, so I had the "Boomigator" lower the boom to indicate we would have fuel for him and got ready for an emergency off-load since he was already in Contact Position. My Boomer reminded me that the F-105 only had an 1 ½ inch manifold and too much pressure would blow him off the boom, so I only planned on using the Forward A/R pump so that our normal 2-pump refueling rate of 3500 lbs-per-minute would be cut in half. I also checked the fuel panel to be sure we could drain some Center Wing fuel forward to keep our center of gravity within limits. I was doing all this from the right seat since the A/C was resting aft. Since we were on the northbound leg of our refueling orbit at the time, I didn't want to turn south until our receiver was on the boom and taking fuel. About this time, I saw the amber Contact Light on my panel and turned on the Forward Refueling Pump. The Aircraft Commander came forward and asked, "What the hell I was doing?" I told him to sit down, shut up and keep his feet off the seat—I had it under control. He was all excited that we could be going into North Vietnam and said, "We could get shot down up here!" By this time I was able to start a gentle 180 degree turn back to the South and back to "friendly" territory. I asked, "How's he doing back there?" I heard, "The fuel's coming out of him about as fast as it's going into him." We were able to keep him on the boom long enough to drag him to "CHARLIE", the homing beacon close to his home base and he was able to "dead-stick" into Khorat RTAFB. At this point, the A/C for the day took over and we returned to U-Tapao—mission complete. I was unsure whether I would receive an "Atta-Boy" or a reprimand, but we did receive a commendation letter from the F-105 Squadron Commander for saving one of his assets. When I was Base Ops Officer at McConnell in 1974, I ran into the "other" Aircraft Commander on that mission. He came into my "realm"—Base operations—and I asked him if he received his Air Medal for that mission. He said, "I hate to tell you this, Bob, but I got the DFC.

I really liked the KC-135 mission when we were flying out of U-Tapao. We weren't refueling the B-52s that were also stationed there. We were doing what I considered the most important mission in Thailand, refueling the F-4 fighter-bombers out of Ubon and Udorn plus the F-105s out of Tahkli and Khorat. These guys were the real "Yankee Air Pirates", as some were termed. We would wait in a refueling anchor until called to "top-off" Ford Flight, Chevy Flight, Olds Flight, or whichever was just out of their base and heading up north during the Linebacker II, missions that had finally been authorized to drive the North Vietnamese to the conference table. The receivers would check in on Refueling frequency, zoom in to pre-contact position, and without any fuss or fanfare, cycle through the refueling in less than 15 minutes for all 4 in the flight and be on their way to drop their loads of 250, 500s or 750s on bridges, rail yards, missile sites or anti-aircraft gun emplacements. We would loiter for 30 or 45 minutes awaiting the return for post-mission refueling on the way back. It was always a thrill when lead called for check-in and we heard, "2,3,4." Only once did we not hear all four checking in. All we heard was, "2----4, and 3 bought it."

I don't know if the B-52s out of U-Tapao ever had to refuel, but I knew one of the "BUFF" Aircraft Commanders, a fraternity brother of mine from Washington University, who told me, "I'm sick and tired of bombing women and children in downtown Hanoi!" I told him, "Either get over it or get out of the Air Force!"

I still had some 60-1 requirements (qualification/annual) to fulfill in the KC-135 before I could complete my two year tour in SAC. Therefore, I was scheduled for a local mission to fill the squares to remain current, to include 3 non-precision and 2 precision approaches and a full stop landing. The weather in Wichita was almost winter-like, cold with low clouds and occasional rain. We took off for a scheduled four hour local mission and began our ups and downs around Mc Connell AFB and the surrounding Kansas territory. The weather at altitude was clear blue above a 3500-4000 ft. deck of clouds. As I descended on the outbound leg of a VORTAC approach, I entered the top of the clouds, turned on the engine heat and began the turn to final approach course inbound. That was when I noticed that ice was beginning to build up on the engine nacelles and leading edges of the wings. The closer to the runway I flew, the more the ice built up, the heavier we became and the more our stall speed increased. By the time we started our go-around, the ice was thick, we were heavy and the power was a little slow on response to the throttles. When we were back on top, in the sunshine, the ice broke off and everything was back to normal. Before I did that again, I called the Command Post and said the conditions weren't good, that I was icing up each time I entered the clouds and I thought it was time to quit.

However, "Charlie" had no such qualms and ordered me to keep it up until my 4 hours were up and I had my required procedures completed. The second descent and long approach was even more precarious, with ice build-up even more severe. We were even heavier and the stall speed had increased another 10%. After our missed approach and go-around, the ice again peeled off by sublimation, but I decided to petition the "Powers that be" to put an end to this foolishness and call it a day. The Command Post, in typical SAC fashion, said that we'd be able to land after the 3rd non-precision approach. So, up, up and away I went for more fun in the freezing rain, which by this time, had caused the cloud tops to rise above 7000 feet. I was told by Approach Control that I couldn't expect my next approach time until a KC-135 inbound ahead of me had landed. As I listened to the other's approach, the A/C remarked that the ceiling and visibility was coming down close to minimums and that he was picking up ice on final approach. Weather confirmed that the temperature and dew point were both near the freezing point. When it came to my turn to commence my final approach, I called for landing data and was informed that there was ice on the runway and the RCR (Runway Condition Reading) was very low. About this time, The Command Post called and reported that Captain Callens had just landed and had not been able to turn off the runway. He had tried to exit, but had slid off the taxiway and had the tail overhanging the runway. My next order, instead of go around and wait until the runway is clear, was,

"Go to Minot, Jackes. Call here when you get there!" So, we looked up the direction and distance to North Dakota, figured our fuel remaining and headed north. When we arrived at Minot AFB, the Command Post had coordinated our arrival. We were met by Transient Alert and parked in front of Base Ops. It was late and as soon as we secured quarters, the only place still open for a meal was the Base Bowling Alley, where we could have a burger and fries at least. Having been stranded away from home before in B-50s and C-47s, I at least had some survival gear (tooth brush, etc.) in my helmet bag. The next morning, the Command Post cleared us to come home since the runway had been cleared of the derelict KC-135 as well as the ice. We landed without further incident—I even quashed the urge to remind them that I had warned them about the icing—"I told you so!" wouldn't have set too well with my bosses. Now that we were free to venture home, we retrieved our vehicles from the squadron parking lot. Some of the crewmembers had trouble starting or entering their cars, but I opened up my Gremlin and it started right up. I was feeling pretty good about that until my overheat light came on and I had to pull into the Base Service Station before my radiator blew. As I sat there, waiting for my radiator to thaw out, I watched the other crewmembers file past—shades of Watertown.

CHAPTER 16

BACK IN '47 (BUT YOU WERE ONLY 10)

C-That Is

After two years of a very satisfying career in KC-135s, I was finally able to get out of SAC and back into Tactical Air Command and my beloved Gooney Bird. I had volunteered to go back to Southeast Asia—anything to get out of SAC. Refueling is a great way to make a living, if you don't have to do it in SAC. You have all the responsibility and no authority.

So now it was back to England AFB to requalify in the C-47 after two years in 4-engine jets. I guess TAC figured that I had forgotten my good habits or had picked up some bad ones in SAC. Therefore, I had to go through a requalification course. This was like a vacation to me, back in Louisiana for 2 or 3 weeks. The flying was fun since I had been an IP and FE for two years in Taiwan. Along with the required proficiency items and emergency procedures, most of the missions were just plain fun and the "Instructor" and I would swap lies and tell tales about what happened when this failed or about that wild weather we had encountered or about Vietnam. One of the last days was spent sight-seeing around Baton Rouge and landing at Monroe for lunch before refueling and returning to Alexandria for a simulated single-engine ILS approach with a full stop landing. It was good to "come home" to my old familiar Gooney Bird and the friendly confines of England AFB. When I processed out with my Training Record, the NCO who signed me out said, "Captain, I never saw anybody come through here with all 5's before." I replied that he had probably never seen anybody come through here with 3500 hours in the airplane, either.

Before I headed west for another tour in Southeast Asia, I dropped by Randolph AFB to visit the USAF Personnel Center to discuss my future in the Air Force. I finally found who I was seeking and we sat down to look over my Air Force Personnel Record. After some serious perusal, my Career Advisor leaned back, looked me in the eye and said, "Well, lad, you have career progression, but it's going in the wrong direction." He showed me my last 3 OERs (Officer Efficiency Rating) from Taiwan and after. I had progressed from a 9/4 (the highest) to an 8/3 (ugh) to a 7/2 (almost bottom) in 3 years. After I digested this bad news, he offered a dire suggestion, "I advise you to find another way to make a living."

The next item on my 1973 agenda was a Jungle Survival School, one of which I had already survived in Panama as an Air Commando before going to Vietnam. This one was conducted at Clark AFB in the Philippines, one of my favorite places in the Far East. During the first day of classroom orientation, we were introduced to "Susie", a huge Bushmaster about 12 feet long that none of us had noticed in the back of the classroom until "she" was pointed out to us. It was a little spooky having that creature with us there, but we were assured that there was no danger if we left her alone. Nobody had to be told that twice. Now it was time to put our school learning to practice actually out in the jungle. We were flown out to a remote clearing by CH-53 helicopter and dropped off for our 3-day survival trial, which included learning how to hollow out a bamboo limb to make a rice cooker, what plants one could eat, how to find water from a hanging vine and the fact that, if we were captured by the local Indian tribesmen who would be looking for us, we should surrender our hat to them without resistance since each hat collected by the hunters represented a pound of rice for them and for some of them, that was their livelihood, so don't argue with them. Besides, none of them spoke English. Before we were sent out into the jungle to hide and evade capture, we were given a little demonstration of how to make a good hiding place with very little effort by using the natural terrain for cover. There were 4 or 5 of the local tribesmen there in front of us and we were told to make a large circle around them. They were going to hide and we were to see if we could find them. We all stood in that circle with our backs to the center for what seemed only a minute or so. Then the Instructor told us to turn around and begin looking for them. We fanned out in an ever increasing pattern until we were called back to the starting area, about ten minutes later. Nobody in our group had seen or heard anything that would give us a clue as to where the Indians had gone into hiding. As we all stood around perplexed and expectant, the Instructor called the evaders to come out. We were astounded when they popped up right at our feet. They had been there the whole time and we had no clue as to how they had fooled us. I'm sure none of us learned to hide that fast or that well.

When it came our turn the next day to escape and evade capture by the now invisible hunters, we all took off in different directions. This was our third day out in the "Bush" and we were tired, sweaty and hungry, but each was determined to not be the one to lose his hat. I had found what looked like a suitable hiding spot along the side of a steep embankment and burrowed in under a large log and pulled as many leaves around me as I could without making an obvious pile. I was making love to that hillside and log cover when I felt a tap on my shoulder and there he was with his hand out. As I handed it to him I asked, "How you find?" He didn't answer of course but he merely pointed to his nose, then to me and ran off.

I was off to Thailand again and my new job with my old aircraft, this time with the 432 TAC Fighter/Recon Wing. The wing consisted of 144 F-4s and 1 Gooney Bird, plus a T-29, tail number 038, which I called "the Great 38". It was grey with a white top with UNITED STATES OF AMERICA in blue letters on the white background. It was the VIP aircraft and flew to a lot of exotic places with Generals and State/Defense Department officials, while I merely "putzed" around in my camouflaged tail-dragger with a cute cartoon on the nose of Snuffy Smith's baby boy, "Tater II".

One day, I went to a staff meeting in the Wing Commander's office, when someone mentioned "the C-47". "What C-47?" "That one, there on the ramp." "Do we own that C-47?" At this point, I introduced myself as the IP, SEFE, PCP etc. of the lowly Gooney Bird. I was sure he had never flown on it.

Some of the F-4 pilots had to attend a tactics conference in Bangkok and after a week of fighter tactics and "fun", they required an airlift home. So who was going to airlift these "Yankee Air Pirates", as the North Vietnamese called American pilots? Call Airlift Ops—me— and schedule its most available C-47 pilot—me—to go down to BKK and fly these F-Warriors" back to the 432nd TFW. I easily made the trip down and loaded 15 or so hangovers into my "Douglas Racer" for the 45 minute trip back.

"The missions never over 'til the paperwork's complete." Signing off the 781 after my last mission at Udon RTAB, 1973.

About 30 minutes after take-off, at 7000 feet, I was almost in sight of UDN. I called Approach Control and asked for a lower altitude. I was cleared to 6000 feet. With the airfield right on the nose, I cancelled IFR (Instrument Flight Rules) and was cleared to Udon Tower. I requested a 360 Degree overhead pattern just like the F-4s would do. I was cleared to "Report Initial at 1 mile. I put the nose down, aimed for the end of the runway and had the airspeed up to 160 knots at 2000 feet, called 1 mile initial. "Report the break" I was told. As I crossed the field boundary, I called the break, retarded the throttles to IDLE, which caused the gear warning horn to wail, pitched out at 150 and pulled 3 or 4 G's through the 60° degree bank into a 180° degree turn while calling, "Gear Down". The co-pilot said, "We're too fast, the gear won't come down." As we slid through 120, the gear came down nicely and he locked it in place. I was rolling to final when I called, "Flaps full." Again, he thought we were still too fast, but put the flap handle to full down. Below 105, the flaps deployed fully, we slowed to 90, 85 75 and I touched down on the numbers fairly smoothly, and turned off at the next taxiway. Immediately, I heard 30 hands clapping and a chorus of "Shit Hot's!" from the back. After shut down and turn to parking spot—in that order- I heard a Major say, "I didn't know you could do that with a Gooney Bird." I replied, "You can do anything except fly fast or go high." That night, I couldn't buy a drink at the O. Club.

Also carrying passengers around Thailand, was a pair of T-39s, call sign SCATBACK. They flew VIPs out of Tan Son Nhut AB in Vietnam and usually base-hopped around Thailand visiting Ubon, Udon, Khorat, NKP and Tahkli, the primary fighter, bomber, tanker and recce bases. The T-39 pilots were authorized to wear grey, short sleeved flight suits, even though they flew air conditioned, pressurized twin jets at FL310 and True Airspeed of 460. We, on the other hand, flew low, slow and sweaty. We were finally approved to have locally made flight suits of light weight gabardine with short sleeves and squadron patches in green color so we at least not get soaking wet while on the ground in the USAF "green bags" that were standard issue, and HOT. At least we looked more professional to the passengers—and at the bar at the O. Club. We were allowed to have "party Suits" made by the same off-base tailor, Amarjit the "Thief", as he was known. Mine was (is) charcoal red double knit and blended in with all those of the F-4 folks, except that mine had (has) a white C-47 embroidered on the back with the words: "REAL AVIATORS FLY TAILDRAGGERS". I didn't mix well with the fighter/recce "pukes" when I wore my party suit. I even had it altered, so after 40 years, I can still fit into it. I attended a Udon RTAB reunion In 2013, thinking that was what to wear to such an affair. I was the only one at the Wright--Patterson AFB Club in a party suit and nobody knew what it was, but I was the only pilot there. At least, my green flight suit was recognized at the Air Force Museum as well as at the Thai restaurant in downtown Dayton the night before.

The flying in Thailand consisted mostly of the daily round-robin from Udon to Khorat to Don Muang (Bangkok) to Phitsanoluk to Lampang to Chiang Mai and return to Udon. I was also responsible for giving check rides and upgrades to other pilots in the Airlift Section. At the same time, I wrote a 100 question proficiency exam based on all the information in the C-47 Flight Manual (Dash -1). I didn't find such an exam within the section, so I made one up, submitted it to 13th Air Force, had it approved and administered to almost all the C-47 pilots for the "Mini Over SEA Airline". Whenever a new procedure or checklist item or change came in, I had to post it and see that each pilot had the new material in his mission kit. (Ten years later, I would be producing such updates to FLIP (Flight Information Publications) through the Pacific Branch of Defense Mapping Agency.)

"Summertime, and the flying was easy". However, in the summertime and fall, the local farmers would burn off the stubble left after a rice harvest and we would see weather observations of "Clear, Visibility 1/4 mile and haze. Sometime, we could only see the first runway marker as we lined up for takeoff. Other than that, the weather was very seldom a problem.

While the F-4s were bombingup North, without my KC-135 support, I was carrying passengers and cargo around Thailand as well as volunteering to fly the unmarked C-47 of the DEPCHIEFUSMAGTHAI, actually, a CIA asset. When I flew it, twice, I had to wear civilian clothes, a safari suit in my case, also made in Thailand, with no military ID. Hanging out with the Air America folks at their club on the West side of Udon, I met a lovely lady who worked for DEPCHIEF, Nancy, who taught me to play Cribbage, but who drove me crazy. She was so aloof and had a fighter pilot Major for a boy-friend that I thought I'd never make any time with her. I finally had an opportunity to impress her when I unexpectedly saw a pair of red shoes behind my elevator after I landed DEPCHIEF's C-47 at Vientianne Laos for a passenger pick-up and return to Udon. I casually walked around the tail and when she saw me, she said, "Well, Mr. Jackes, what brings you here?" I merely replied, as cooly as my racing heart would allow, "I just came to pick you up and take you home." After boarding and a super smooth take off, my boss, who was in the right seat for this mission, said, "Why don't you bring your "girlfriend" up here and let her sit here for landing?" When she was settled in the right seat, I showed her how to lower the landing gear and flaps which she did nicely as we turned final approach for Udon. It was about 5 PM, very little wind, and the sun setting looked like a Japanese painting in the haze. When I touched down, there wasn't a bump, squeak or anything but a whisper. I told her to raise the flaps as I lowered the tail to the runway and turned off to the Air America ramp. When she complimented me on the smooth landing, I merely said, "You didn't think I'd bounce with you on board, did you?" Following that, I managed to play more than Cribbage with her while her major was looking for her.

Another "Number one good deal, GI" was living in air conditioned BOQs with maid and laundry service for 6-man suites with refrigerators. We were close to the O. Club as well as the Base Pool and close enough to the front gate that one could easily walk to Amarjiit's and the Golden Palm Thai Restaurant. The bus stop was just outside the main gate also for an occasional trip to the popular downtown watering hole, The Yellow Bird.

One of my missions flying around Thailand involved a stop at Bangkok for the on-load of some very special cargo destined eventually for the O. Club at Udon. It was several cases of booze to be served at a General's retirement party, The General's aide was aboard this flight in order to assure it was transferred from the MAGTHAI Class 6 store to our waiting transport at Don Muang and carried the rest of the way around the circuit to Udon. Unfortunately, after our stop in Phitsanoluk, we were heading East around the murky gloom of southern Laos, when I noticed the RPM on No. 2 engine was winding down and told Bill Pelfrey that we were going to have to shut it down and return to Phitsanoluk while declaring an emergency. We turned into the late afternoon sun after securing No. 2 and stated our intention of landing on one engine back at PTL. Since Bill was not real familiar with the C-47, I had to handle the emergency landing myself, but couldn't see far enough ahead in the moderate to violent haze to be sure when I could descend to the runway. Fortunately, we had our Terminal Approach Procedure handy and managed to make a VOR straight-in approach in about ½ mile visibility. Everyone was relieved to say the least when we touched down and rolled off to the ramp on the right before shutting down the good engine. While the Flight Mechanic checked to see what had happened to the other engine and give us the bad news that we were going to be stuck there for a while, the General's aide was frantically looking for another way to get his precious cargo to its destination. For our part, we were able to arrange for a CH-3 helicopter to come and pick us up and return us to Udon. The engine could be fixed fairly easily with just a cylinder change, which the CH-3 had brought with it, but we weren't going to stay until that was completed. Evidently, the General's Aide found some Thai Army troops to guard the booze while he waited for maintenance to fix the broken bird. I don't remember how I made it back to retrieve the airplane, but it certainly wasn't on a CH-3. That is the only time I want to be in the back of that noisy flying machine. When Bill and I jumped off, we couldn't hear each other, our ears were ringing so. (My ears still ring 40 years later). Anyway, I managed to return and finish our round-robin on two good engines. The Aide was very glad to see us after a worrisome night and was happy to be going home. When we settled on the UDN parking ramp, I remarked that I would certainly like to sample some of that booze, but I wasn't invited to the party. He said, "Look behind your seat, Captain—I took care of you." Then I retrieved a Demi-John of Courvoissier wrapped in cellophane. It was more than I expected and I took good care of it until I was able to get it back to my BOQ. I put it up on the top of a clothes locker and kind of forgot about it until one day I went to have a little nip of post-mission whiskey. When I took it down, I saw that it was only about 1/3 full (or 2/3s empty) and was going to accuse the maids/laundresses of piracy. They certainly had access because they were around all day doing their chores and cooking fish heads and rice in the hallway. About this time I decided to lock it up so they couldn't get to it, one of my suite-mates confessed that he had been the culprit. After working all night in the Radar Bomb-Scoring Unit, tracking the B-52s on long-range radar, he would come home while we were asleep and after the Club was closed and help himself to a nip or two out of my big and expensive Demi-John without my ever noticing it. He was a lush anyway, divorced and serving his last tour as a B-52 IP before separating from SAC—even faster than I did.

The day I discovered this was "the morning after". I used to like to go to the Club on Tuesday nights because the menu included fried chicken, all-you-can-eat, a delightful sparkling Rose wine and Thai kick-boxing. There was a boxing ring set up alongside the patio dining area where some 5, 6, and 7 year old Thai kids would kick the stuffing out of each other for our entertainment. After an enjoyable night of chicken, wine and kick- boxing, I made it back to the Q and to bed just in time to be roused after an hour or so for an emergency mission. It seemed that the SAC Major's RBSU had gone toes up, "tits up" in our vernacular, and the only replacement part was at Ubon. Could I fly my magic Gooney Bird down to Ubon and bring back this critical part so that the bomb-scorers could get back in business? Sure I could do that, and since it was too early for a hangover, I took off and headed down the road at about 4 in the morning. Just as I was looking to find the base, about 6 AM, the sun was coming up, directly in front of my nose, making it almost impossible to see anything on the ground. Back to the Terminal Approach book and another instrument approach. As soon as I taxied to the ramp, without shutting down, someone handed the Crew Chief the box containing $10,000 worth of electronics, and we were off, back to Udon, thankfully with the sun behind us. I was back in the BOQ by 7:30 and that's when I hit the Courvoissier bottle.

HAVE GOONEY WILL TRAVEL

CAPT. P.R. JACKES, PCP, FCF, IP, SEFE
MINI AIRLINES, UDORN

That's me and my calling card at Udorn Royal Thai Air Base in 1973. The initials on the card stand for: Passenger Carrying Pilot, Functional Check Flight, Instructors Pilot, Standardization Evaluation Flight Examiner, all for (MINI) over – (SEA) Airline. I kind of owned that camouflaged beauty.

My year in Thailand wasn't all fun and games. The Red Cross notified me that it was cutting orders for an emergency leave to hurry back to Wood River because my father-in-law was about to die. I arrived there just in time to see him for the last time. He was bloated and jaundiced and died the next day on Easter.

About four months later, I received another set of emergency leave orders to return to St. Louis because my mother was close to death from cancer. My trip home was easy until we departed Hawaii on TIA, Trans-International Airways, a contract carrier which was flying a DC-8 to the States. It developed an emergency, smoke in the cockpit, right after departing Honolulu International. So, we returned to Honolulu to fix the problem. After some Martinis in the terminal bar, we re-boarded and headed East again. Upon our approach to California, the pilot announced that he was landing at Oakland International rather than Travis AFB due to the maintenance problem that could be handled by TIA's own maintenance facility there at Oakland. Therefore, I had to ride over to San Francisco rather than catch a military hop out of Travis to Scott AFB in Illinois, this caused me to land at St. Louis International and have my wife pick me up there. By the time we arrived at Barnes Hospital, I was informed that it was too late, my mother had passed away before I could see her for the last time. Thank you, TIA!

The last call from the Red Cross was in early December and it bade me to return because my wife was near death with Emphysema at Wood River Hospital and had no one to care for our 5 year old. This was going to be my third trip home with only 2 or 3 weeks left on my tour in

SEA, so I told them that I wasn't coming back just to pack up and return anyway. So Roy Preece was good enough to pack up my meager belongings and sent them to Wood River via Scott AFB. When I arrived in Wood River, I immediately went to the hospital within sight of our house and visited my wife. She was on oxygen so she could breathe, but said she wanted a cigarette. I told her that she couldn't have one because of the oxygen and the fact that they had probably put her in that condition—she should quit now. She said, "I'd rather die rather than quit smoking." I said that that was a fine thing to say in front of our 5-year old.

My tour as Base Operations Officer at McConnell AFB in Wichita KS was much different from my brief tour as a KC-135 driver—no alerts, for one thing—and no flying either, except for the Aero. Club and its *NAVION*. Fortunately, I had a very savvy NCOIC who did most of the required duties, so all I had to do is drive the Air Force blue station wagon with the red light on top so I could check all the runways, taxiways and ramps for possible FOD (Foreign Object Damage), including the one over at the Boeing Plant on the West side of the base. Therefore, my job wasn't too demanding, which allowed plenty of time to find other diversions—like Becky Crane.

Becky was a large, lovely lady who I met at one of my favorite watering holes, the Leopard Spot, which was right outside the back gate of McConnell. She and I had many good times together. In fact, I even talked her into joining the Air Force, which I did right after I took her for a short ride in the *NAVION*. This airplane, similar to the T-34 at England AFB, was fun to fly but had a peculiarity in the gear system that allowed the landing gear to creep down during flight due to a slight hydraulic leak and merely required the pilot to re-raise the gear when it crept down and the airspeed began to decrease.

I used to enjoy cruising the ramps first thing in the duty day. One morning, my staff car was completely covered with ice. While contemplating my dilemma, I noticed a transient F-100 starting up on the ramp in front of Base Ops. What better way to defrost a vehicle than to pull up behind a J-57 engine and let the jet exhaust do the defrosting for me? In 10 seconds, the deed was done and I shut off the defroster to keep the kerosene fumes out of my now-dry car and proceeded on my way.

Another job of the Base Ops Officer was reviewing and adjusting the Hurricane Evacuation procedures. Since McConnell was smack in the middle of the country, it was an ideal location for any aircraft stationed near the eastern or southern coasts to which to evacuate ahead of a hurricane. I had to assure that all the taxiways, parking ramps and hangar aprons would be available for transient aircraft parking. This also included the large ramp of the Boeing facility whenever it was not taken up by large Boeing aircraft, like the two ex-PANAM 747s that had been stationed there during a monstrous thunderstorm during which, both aircraft sustained over a million Dollar's-worth of damage from the ensuing hail storm. The plan also called for maximum use of the Base Motor Pool to supply busses and "bread Trucks" for aircrew transportation. The Clubs, dining hall and housing facility had to be in the coordination process as well. I only had to exercise the plan once when a hurricane threatened the Gulf States and all the training aircraft from Columbus AFB in Mississippi came for a two-day visit. The plan worked just fine since we didn't have any large transport or bomber aircraft to bed down.

I enjoyed checking out the Boeing Plant and its huge hangar, the biggest building on the field. I managed to wangle a guided tour through it one day so I could witness the Stress Test Evaluation on the B-52 that was tethered therein. The engineers had covered most of the wing areas, tail section and some of the fuselage with a maze of wires that would read out the stress pressure at a myriad of points while the mechanical "jig" in which it was confined simulated actual flying conditions, including take off, turbulence, extreme maneuvers and landing. The test mechanism could simulate an 8-hour mission profile in less than an hour's time. Whenever a stress fracture occurred, it was recorded by the system and photographed. It's no wonder the B-52 is still flying 40 years later.

Checking out the Boeing side of the field also availed me of the opportunity to drop into the Leopard Spot, where I could be served by the lovely Becky Crane, the long-legged

Amazon who I liked to visit. That was what I was doing, off-base, the night McConnell had its first and only fatal tanker crash.

Returning to the BOQ early one morning, I was informed that all kinds of people had been looking for me and that I needed to report to the scene of the KC-135 crash off the end of the runway. I was reluctant to explain my absence during the event, but asked, "What do you think I could have done?" The tanker had crash-landed right between the runways at Cessna and Beechcraft just north of the McConnell parallel runways. By the time I arrived, there was nothing left but a smoking hole in the ground, the main gear trucks and the steel-banded tail section. The sight of it made me glad I hadn't been there when the crash happened.

CHAPTER 17

SCOTT AFB – AS AN E-4

Since I had been ordered by President Nixon to resign my commission, I decided to go home and look for "another way to make a living" as my Career Advisor had recommended. I lived only 22 miles from Scott AFB and there were airplanes there, so I decided to visit Military Airlift Command Personnel and see if I could find a job there. I knew I was going to have to start at the bottom but I knew I wanted to do it with a flying organization. When the sergeant put the newly-printed organizational roster in front of me, I asked, "Which ones fly airplanes?" He told me the 11th AAS (Aeromedical Airlift Squadron) did and I said, "That's for me!" Then he cut orders assigning me as an E-4 Air Operations Specialist, 70210, and sent me to my new assignment. So, I took my new assignment orders to the 11th AAS and was introduced to the Commander, Lt. Col Jack Compton, as his new Ops Specialist. I saluted the

Commander and was welcomed to the C-9 Squadron. Next, I met the Ops Officer, a Major, with whom I became friends after 3 years and 3 promotions. I also found out that I had more flying time than anyone in the squadron except him and the Sqdn Cmdr. The fact that I had been an Officer for 14 ½ years was not going to make any difference as far as my job assignment was concerned. For the next 6-8 months, I found out what all the Airmen and Sergeants did while I was out flying airplanes. I was now the "hired help" who had to learn how to scrub and polish floors, clean windows and sills, empty ash trays, rake and mow the surrounding squadron grass, etc. During preparation for an upcoming CFI (Commander's Facility Inspection) by HQ Military Airlift Command (MAC), I was working on scraping the old wax off the linoleum floor tile when I met the "Old Man" also on his hands and knees doing the same thing. That was a great incentive to forget my previous grades and do my best for the 11th AAS. We passed the inspection with ease.

Following my first promotion to E-5 in 1975, I had to assume more responsibility. I had taken my first WAPS (Weighted Airman Promotion System) test and couldn't believe how basic and fundamental the test had been, but after 14 ½ years of flying and leadership positions in all parts of the World plus four years of college, the questions seemed rather mundane. Evidently, I had pretty well aced my first test and early one morning, I received a phone call from the Sqdn Cmdr before heading out the door in Wood River, that I was now a Staff Sergeant instead of an Airman First Class—congratulations and all that. When I reported to the squadron, the Commander called me into his office, handed me my new rank insignia and said that I was now his new Ops NCO. Now I had to complete all the mandatory training classes to become a competent NCO. These included: MANAGEMENT 1, COURSE FOR AIR FORCE SUPERVISORS (50 hours), 1975 as a Staff sergeant, HUMAN COMMUNICATIONS WORKSHOP, 1976, AIR FORCE WRITING COURSE, 1976, TRAINER/SUPERVISOR ORIENTATION, 1976, AIR FORCE WRITING COURSE, 1976, EQUIPMENT CUSTODIAN, 1976, OJT ADMINISTRATOR ORIENTATION, 24 hours, 1977 and SUPERVISOR SAFETY COURSE VIII as a TSGT in 1977. All this education would allow me to progress from a lowly E-4 in '74 to E-5 in '75 to E-6 in '76. Of course, having 15 plus years in the Air Force and having 6800 hours flying time in 7 or 8 countries and about 10 states kind of gave me an edge.

Now it was time to prove my worth. Enter the computer age and MACARMS—Military Airlift Command Aircrew Resource Management System, into which I entered on the ground floor in 1976. If not on the ground floor, at least just up the stairs, which was appropriate since the offices for the Commander, Ops Officer and pilots were on the 2nd floor.

MACARMS was one of the USAF's attempts to

computerize the records maintenance and scheduling of all airlift aircrews. By the time it was ready to be implemented, we administrators had already been introduced to IBM punch card decks and many, many editions of the ensuing printouts that we retrieved from the mainframe building next door that housed the hardware for the system. On a particular Friday afternoon, we scavenged all the hand-written schedules and mission histories and replaced them with the most current, computer-generated printouts for aircrew scheduling. It was almost comical on Monday morning to see and hear the schedulers looking for their carefully maintained schedules and looking at the pile of printer paper sitting in the middle of their desks. A chorus of "Where are all our schedules and records?" was answered by "Right in front of you. From now on, the Flight Orders will be produced by computer and all flying times and accomplishments will be input through this terminal by our Ops NCO"—me. Each Scheduler had his/her own computer terminal and now received detailed instruction from the two Officers that had established the system and had worked the "kinks" out of it after many months of trial and error. I had learned a lot from them—in fact, everything I ever knew about computers. (It was also a plus that one of them was a cute 1st Lt. She eventually went to Shemya Alaska where her life changed rather dramatically—another story.)

One of my daily duties was to input all the flight data

from the previous day's missions into the MACARMS data base gathered from the 781s, the flight logs of flying time and accomplishments, including instrument approaches, day hours or night hours that the pilots were required to make to maintain currency. After a month or two of repetition, I was able to take Burris to work with me so he could see what I did and how I did it. Since he had such an interest in computers, even as early as 7 years old, I started to teach him how to do the job of data input. He was all dressed up in his plaid shorts and a white fringed leather jacket. He was standing at my terminal doing what I had taught him, when Capt. Mulkey came over and asked him if he could use the machine. Burris looked up at him and said" "I'm busy, inputting flying history!" I thought the Captain was going to fall down laughing, especially when he realized that Burris actually <u>was</u> putting in flying history.

I had acquired a red '66 *Chevelle* convertible upon my return from my final tour at Mc Connell. It had bucket seats, a floor-mounted shifter and a 327 cu.in. V-8 engine, one of three that would be installed during its short life. I had also found a "shade-tree" mechanic who was able to put a nice mellow set of duals on it and change the transmission to a 4-speed manual with a Hurst Shifter. He also replaced the first 327 after the original had swallowed a valve, and the second when it went "toes-up" with a hole in the piston. Both were rebuilds, but my favorite engine and easy to install. It was a hot buggy and I enjoyed my morning drive to Scott AFB, sometimes with the top down, but I enjoyed my 2 or 3 hour drive home even more. I took a different route to Wood River every day depending on which bars I wanted to hit on the way home. I knew every bar from Belleville to Alton, including some in Collinsville, Caseyville on Route 4, 157 and 159 as well as 111 if I were going as far as Alton.

The Squadron had some promotion parties at Scott and, of course, I was in attendance for most of them. For the DO's (Director of Operations) promotion, the party was held at a local farm just a mile around the corner from the Base where a 1st Lt., a C-9 Pilot, rented his bachelor pad. This party was in the late summer and the corn was high on the farm allowing the guests to play a game during which one was challenged to run 20 or 30 yards, put the bat handle on the ground, put ones forehead on top, spin around it 10 times, then pick up the bat and run back to the starting line. Nobody completed the test without veering in the direction of the spin, crashing into the cornfield to much applause and laughter. I think I ended up 3 rows into the 7' tall corn stalks just like everybody else.

Some additional entertainment was provided by a Captain's wife who taught belly-dancing. About 9:00, we were all seated around a camp fire when music started and this gorgeous lady in see-through pants, a beaded halter top and nothing in between but an undulating belly-button began gyrating to the melodic beat and dancing around in front of our wide-eyed circle. Just before the end of the dance, I heard a bachelor Lieutenant exclaim, "I think I'm in Love!"

Our Squadron Ops Officer lived rather close to the Base and would occasionally have a party of his own. He lived on LUCIA LANE in a charming, tastefully decorated house with a patio, a back yard and a small pond about 1/4 acre in size and maybe 4' deep. He also had a boat in his yard, a row boat, lying upside down by the pond's edge. The name of this boat was the LUCIA-TANIA.

One party in particular caused the demise of my "sexy" *Chevelle* and nearly my career. This party was in Belleville at a friend's house and at the end of the night, I stayed around to help my friend clean up and load the dishwasher. By the time I started home, it was already 1 AM and I had a long way to go to return to Wood River via Ill. Rte. 111. I must have dozed off for a second or two, because all of a sudden there was a blacked-out Lincoln stopped in the road just before it divided into 4 lanes going past the 3 oil refineries in Wood River. There was no way I was going to stop in time before I slammed into the back of the dark sedan which had just "T-boned" the car in front of it. Fortunately, the old man driving the Lincoln had already cleared the rear bumper as he was going to attend to his wife in the passenger seat after his crash or I would have cut him off at the knees. My injuries were slight. I chipped off half of a front tooth on the steering wheel and skinned my shins under the dashboard, but the Chevy was toast. While the cops called for a couple of tow trucks and escorted me to an ambulance, they seemed more concerned with my bleeding mouth than they were about my driving condition. I also found out about the cause of the wreck was the fact that some guy driving south had decided to make a U-turn at the divide and did so right in front of the old couple in the Lincoln that hit him broadside right. He didn't have any injuries either, but the fault was laid at his feet and he was arrested. After I was released from Wood River Hospital, my wife came over and took me home. I worried more about my crumpled car than about my chipped tooth. I called my mechanic which had done all the work on it and he just said, "I hope you didn't ruin that nice set of pipes I put on there!" I think they were salvageable, but no more driving the *Chevelle*.

Therefore, I went to my local used car dealer and found a beautiful dark blue Chrysler Cordoba with a white vinyl top. I had had a burgundy Cordoba a year or two before, but these two were the only cars I ever had with automatic transmissions.

Since I had been enlisted for four years, it came to pass that I had to reenlist in 1978 before my upcoming assignment. The Commander and Ops Officer agreed to my request to hold the reenlistment ceremony on a C-9 during a local training mission with some flying time for me. I decided to call the PIO (Public Information Office) and have the event covered in the base newspaper at least. When I called, it went something like this: "I'm going to reenlist aboard a C-9." "We've had lots of people do that." "But, I'm reenlisting for the first time with 18 ½ years total service." The officer who will administer the oath is our first female C-9 pilot, the Certifying Officer just made O-6 (full Colonel)—"still not committed to coverage—" and following the ceremony, this E-6 is going to make 3 touch-and-go's and a full stop landing. "We'll be there."

RED CROSS C-9 – Last, and certainly the least, is the C-9A, a Medical Evaluation version of the DC-9-20 which flew with many airlines and was the most popular commercial airliner in the world, between the DC-3 and the Boeing 737. My last flight was in this aircraft, but not 932, I think it was 656 or 958 with the 11th AAS at Scott AFB in Illinois.

So, here I went, up in the wild blue yonder after 4 ½

years, in an airplane I had never flown before. I took the oath from Susan Rogers, thanked Andy Biancur, both of whom died within two years—cancer and a heart attack—and proceeded to the cockpit for my promised turn at the controls of the C-9-30 with the grey and white paint job and the big red cross on the tail. When my turn to fly came, I jumped into the left seat and was given control. The Instructor briefed me on pattern altitude, airspeeds, flap settings and takeoff checklist items. Then he told me to look at the instrument approach procedure, and prepare for an ILS Approach to RWY 35. Since the Flight Director system was similar to the one I had learned to like in the KC-135 and since it was a beautiful sunny day with very little wind, I had no trouble lining up on the final approach course, flying the glide slope to minimum altitude and landing smoothly just past the numbers. I called for FLAPS-1/4, POWER to MAX, rotated at the required airspeed and climbed out to turn left for a closed pattern. The only problem I had was leveling off at pattern altitude on downwind. The Instructor was following the whole procedure and kept saying, "And level off at 1350 feet—and level off at 1350 feet—AND LEVEL OFF AT 1350—" By pulling off the power sooner and using about 45 degrees of bank, I managed to maintain traffic pattern altitude on the subsequent patterns. I hadn't realized how fast and easy it was to complete the 3 touch-and–go's, but suddenly it was time for my final, full-stop landing, (Shades of my early solos in the T-birds). So much for my flying career—14 ½ years and 6875 hours, but no wreath on my wings.

During my four years as an Enlisted Man, I had the opportunity to meet the legendary "Chappie" James. As Vice Wing Commander under Robin Olds, equally legendary in the annals of air combat, he had devised a plan to conquer the MIG threat over Hanoi and Haiphong. From Ubon RTAFB, in December 1966, Chappie formed a ruse called Operation Bolo whereby he and Olds, as "Blackman" and Robin, would be disguised as F-105 fighter-bombers carrying 750 lb bombs for targets north of the Red River. When the MIGs arose to confront these slow, heavily laden bombers, they found instead 2 flights of F-4 fighters loaded for air-to-air combat. The result was 7 MIGs lost with no losses on the 8th TFW. This was the highest victory total of the Vietnam air war. He had been quoted in <u>Stars and Stripes</u> as having replied to a question about black pilots, "We have no prejudice in my Squadron!"

In 1977, I had my VFW Buddy Poppy donation can and a handful of red poppies out at the base golf course. General (3-star) James had just finished up his round of golf and was in yellow golf slacks and shirt as he entered the club house where I confronted him. I asked, "General, would you care to donate to the VFW Poppy Fund?" I held out my can and offered a poppy. He turned to his white, Captain, aide and said, "Give that man some money, Boy!" I had to control my laughter until I retreated to the parking lot where I guffawed.

CHAPTER 18

SPRECHEN-SIE DEUTCH?

Now it was off to Germany for the last two years of my Air Force career. I was assigned to the Air Liaison Office (ALO) with the 8th Infantry Division. The 8th ID "Pathfinders" was the largest Division in the United States Army. There were 25,000 green uniforms, tanks, armored personnel carriers (APCs) and helicopters and 9 or 10 of us in blue uniforms (except in the field), some Jeeps, radios but no airplanes. I was assigned as the ALO NCO Air Operations Specialist, but I had to learn Office Management from the current NCO and the various Army schools while trying to learn German so I could get along on the local economy.

My first stay and night in Deutchland was spent with my "sponsor" who was only able to pick me up at Rhine-Main International and take me to a local "pension", or a German inn with a bar and restaurant. The first night was a lonely experience. Since I didn't speak any German, I had to order only food that I understood in German—"bifstek und salat." Beer and wine were easy except for which brands were the tastiest. At that point, it didn't matter. The salad was good, but the steak was so rare, I had to chew and chew forever to get it down. By bedtime I was asked if I needed a "heitzung". I had no clue what a "heitzung" was, so I declined. By the next morning, I found myself rolled up into a little ball under the down comforter and didn't want to come out. It was about 45 degrees in that room. I found out later from the proprietor, who spoke very good English, that a heitzung is a heater. I also learned that most Germans know English but won't speak it until you speak, or try to speak, German to them.

So, I started on my German education as well as many courses in Office Management: FILES MAINTENANCE, EQUIPMENT CUSTODIAN TRAINING, the Army way, and SUPERVISORY MANAGEMENT, even though I had no one to supervise or manage. The Air Liaison Officers, a Lt. Col., a Major and a Captain, were all very pleasant and respectful of the fact that I had been an officer and pilot for 14 ½ years. We worked together well, even though we couldn't socialize. When it came time to pick grapes in the local area of Bad Kreutznach, we just shut down the Air Liaison Office and went out to one of the local vineyards in the Nahe Valley to help with the laborious task of bringing in the grape harvest. One of the ALOs, Herr Major Germann, who spoke "Gasthaus Deutch", set me up to pick grapes at a local vineyard owned by a Frau Herfert. Fortunately, I had become friends with the mother of one of our ROMADS (Radio Operator Maintainer and Driver). She was a lovely lady who had been born in Wurtzburg Germany. She agreed to go along with me since I hadn't learned much German. We had to bring our own lunch since the owner lady couldn't afford to provide a noon meal, but we were paid 8 Marks an hour plus 2 bottles of wine a day. Here, for 5 straight days, I learned about "trauben-schneiden, de Kleine Immer, de Grosse Immer plus what back-breaking labor is involved in snipping the bunches of grapes from the vine, placing them in our own little buckets before a worker with a great big bucket on his back came down the row so we could dump our crop into his big immer so he in turn could dump his load into the dumpster on the tractor-drawn wagon that eventually went to the crusher at the winery. All week, Rose kept up a conversation with the nearby pickers and translating most of it for me. We were really relieved when the work ended, but had a lot of fun together that week.

One of my fondest diversions during my two year unaccompanied tour in Germany was *Volksmarching*. Almost every Saturday I would follow the directions on the current announcement of the closest walking event; This meant driving all over Southeastern Germany in my little Opel two-door to each small town that was sponsoring a Volksmarch. Once I found it, I would sign in, pay my $5 entry fee, eschewing the IVV stamp in my log book because I didn't walk for credit with the International Vander Varung, I just walked 10 kilometers (6.2 miles) for fun and exercise. I would stop at the check points, have my card stamped and sometimes have a brochen or a cup of Gluwine. There was always a gaggle of walkers, some in Leiderhosen and Tyrolahuts,or alpine hats, hiking boots and walking sticks— I still have mine—and we would all take off from the starting point in town and stroll, walk or run through the countryside for about an hour and 20 minutes, have our tickets stamped, collect our medals and then sample the local wine, beer and food. I must have covered about 800 kilometers, or about 500 miles in two years, all in the same pair of sneakers. Now that I live in SE Michigan, I can't find anything resembling Volksmarching. Nobody has even heard of it.

One day I was downtown in Bad Kreutznach at a restaurant and ordered "Viebelkuchen". I thought I had pronounced the onion and egg concoction correctly, remembering the wonderful pie-like creation that Norma Reichart had fixed for me when I was in the 11th Squadron and she was a nurse in the 57th. The waiter responded to my "Viebelkuchen" request with a big "VAS?" I repeated it again but still no understanding. Finally, he said, "You mean 'Sviebelkuchen?" I immediately recognized my mistaken pronunciation and said, "Ya, Ya, Sviebelkuchlen." It still wasn't as good as Nurse Reichert's. The waiter then told me in very good English, "Is besser you speak English."

I had found a little tight golf course in Bad Meunster that was close and fun to play. I had a little trouble keeping my ball out of the wheat fields and vineyards, but I had a good time anyway. In order to improve my game, I asked the manager if I could use the driving range. He then told me, "I have seen you play and I have some advice for you. You leave your voods in de car, Yah? You use only your irons, Yah, and you will do much better." So I did, and I did. Only lost two balls and cut 5 strokes off my score.

My personnel office was located at Sembach AB, an hour south of the 8th Infantry HQ in Bad Kreuznach, so if I had Air Force business, I had to drive there. When it came time to find out what my next assignment was going to be, I visited my Personnel Office to find out what was next. I was offered an assignment to K.I. Sawyer AFB in the UP of Michigan as a Records Clerk or something like that. I immediately asked, "What's my alternative?" The answer was either accept the next assignment or start your retirement. Well, that didn't take long to decide. I immediately went to the personnel specialist and asked to start my retirement processing. This girl was a lot more absorbed with her performance in the USAFE Talent Contest than in this Sergeant's retirement as an O-3. She was scratching her head as she told me, "I knows how to separate people, but I don' know how to retire people." So I told her that WE were going to get into the books and figure out how we were going to start my retirement." Within about three weeks, I had the proper paperwork and returned to my home base, Scott AFB so I could complete my retirement processing which included a train trip to the VA Hospital in Chicago for a retirement physical—a piece of cake, but I was glad that I didn't have any more business with the VA.

So, on 29 April 1980, I retired as a Captain, became a civilian and went home to Wood River to begin my leisure time taking care of my 12 year old son while my wife worked at a law firm in Alton. Now all I had to do was put in my application at Defense Mapping Agency and take the test. After that, I waited for about 8 ½ months until I was notified that I had scored 103 and would start as a GS-7.

That was the beginning of another Satisfying 20 year career and another long story.

Made in USA - Kendallville, IN
86595_9781946746269
04.12.2023 1333